Carnivore Diet Cookbook

2000 Days of Simple & Delicious, Nutrient-Packed Recipes for Beginners with a 30-Day Meal Plan for Weight Loss, Reduced Inflammation & Increased Energy for a Carnivore Lifestyle.

Embrace a Healthy Lifestyle without Sacrificing Flavor.

Emory Stout

TABLE OF CONTENTS

INTRODUCTION..6
CHAPTER 1: UNDERSTANDING THE STRICT
CARNIVORE DIET....................................7
The Basics of the Carnivore Diet: What You
Need to Know..7
Nutritional Benefits of a Meat-Only Diet........8
Common Myths and Misconceptions about
the Carnivore Diet.............................. 10
Key Components: The Staples of a Carnivore
Diet.. 11
The Role of Fat and Protein: Balancing Your
Macros..13
Harnessing Nutrients for Optimal Health on
the Carnivore Diet.............................. 14
CHAPTER 2: 30-DAY MEAL PLAN................. 18
CHAPTER 3: BREAKFASTS: Classic
carnivore breakfasts........................... 21
Supreme bacon and eggs...................... 21
Pork clipping stuffed with cheese.......... 21
Fried mini beef rolls............................ 22
Pork belly breakfast............................ 22
Quail eggs in butter with beef................23
Cheese and egg burrito with steak and
bacon..23
Fish fingers in egg batter with sauce.....24
Cheese and beef muffins......................24
CHAPTER 4: BREAKFASTS: Morning fuel:
quick and delicious breakfasts...................25
Salty cheesecakes with butter..............25
Soft baked eggs.................................25
Cottage cheese mousse.......................26
Beef forshmak................................... 26
Fried egg-breaded chicken fillet............ 27
Quail eggs with carpaccio from smoked
wild salmon.......................................27
Chicken fillet with raw smoked sausage28
Meat soufflé......................................28
CHAPTER 5: BREAKFASTS: Omelettes and
Casseroles...29
Chicken fillet and feta cheese omelet....29
Ham and cheese omelet.......................29
Fish fingers and egg casserole.............30
Egg casserole with chicken minced meat..
30
Chicken fillet in cheese and egg dough.31
Turkey and cheddar casserole.............. 31
CHAPTER 6: BREAKFASTS: Family weekend
breakfasts... 32
Haddock and egg fritters...................... 32
Bacon egg muffins..............................32
Meat joaf with cheese sauce................. 33
Cheese pancakes with boiled egg circles..
33
Turkey tubes with bacon......................34
Cheese soufflé with bacon................... 34
CHAPTER 7: LUNCHES: Savory soups and
best stew recipes................................35
Seafood chowder................................35
Creamy chicken liver soup.................... 35
Cream soup of beef and cheese...........36
Pork belly stew...................................36
Fish stew in clay pot............................37
French cheese soup.............................37
Lamb ragu italian-style........................ 38
Braised beef tongue............................38
CHAPTER 8: LUNCHES: Meat lover's
paradise: pork dishes for everyone............ 39
Stuffed pork zrazy...............................39
Cream pork chops...............................39
Pork minced pockets...........................40
Pork stew..40
Pork roll with chicken and cheese.........41
Pork and lamb kebab with sauce..........41
CHAPTER 9: LUNCHES: Meat lover's
paradise: beef for the picky eaters...............42
Classic roast beef...............................42
Beef stroganoff...................................42
Baked beef in yogurt...........................43
Butter-stuffed beef cutlet.....................43
Cheesy chopped beefsteak...................44
Pepper-crusted beef medallions...........44
CHAPTER 10: LUNCHES: Meat lover's
paradise: quick and easy poultry dishes......45
Crispy chicken tabaka..........................45
Chicken thighs with creamy sauce........45
Chicken fricassee................................46

Fillings from tongue and quail eggs.......46

Speedy chicken fingers............... 47

Stuffed turkey patties............................47

Chicken pudding..............................48

Bacon and cheese stuffed quail............ 48

CHAPTER 11: SNACKS: Quick and tasty snacks.. 49

Beef tartare with cheese....................49

Salmon tartare with egg sauce.............49

Meat boats with eggs.........................50

Chicken julienne................................ 50

Bacon-wrapped shrimp skewers........... 51

Deep-fried pork...................................51

Cheese balls with slices of boiled ham..52

Egg and cheese tacos with meat filling. 52

CHAPTER 12: SNACKS: Salads for everyon 53

Steak and egg salad.........................53

Salad with chicken, shrimp, cheese, and egg...53

Salad with fried pork ham, goat cheese, and poached egg..................................54

Pork chop salad with hard cheese and bacon...54

Variation of the salad "Cobb" with duck breast for Carnivore Diet...................... 55

Cheese salad.......................................55

CHAPTER 13: SNACKS: Homemade broths.56

Beef bone broth...................................56

Chicken bone broth with egg and chicken breast...56

Pork bone broth with meatballs............. 57

Carnivore shurpa without vegetables.... 57

CHAPTER 14: SNACKS: Pates and sauces.. 58

Chicken liver pâté................................58

Béchamel sauce..................................58

Hollandaise sauce...............................59

Peppercorn sauce............................ 59

Béarnaise sauce..................................60

Pork Lard Chimichurri............................60

CHAPTER 15: INSTEAD OF DESSERTS: dairy products for meat-eaters...........................61

Emmental and mascarpone cheesecake.. 61

Milk and ricotta pudding.......................61

Milkshake with cheddar.................... 62

Cottage cheese casserole with cream...62

CHAPTER 16: DINNER: Dishes in one pan...63

Pan-fried shrimp with cheese sauce......63

Roasted beef chunks and beef liver...... 63

Pan-fried pork chunks with meat sauce and quail eggs....................................64

Fish skillet with salmon and bacon........64

CHAPTER 17: DINNER: Meaty dinners for every taste.. 65

Osso buco lamb shank........................65

Herb-crusted rack of lamb.................. 65

Chopped chicken cutlets.......................66

Beef chops with peppercorn sauce....... 66

Beef ham in creamy glaze....................67

Braised pork knuckle............................67

Grilled beef tacos on egg pancakes......68

Stuffed beef patties.............................68

CHAPTER 18: DINNER: Fish dishes for everyday life.. 69

Wild salmon Wellington....................... 69

Seared sea bass with butter and cheese sauce...69

Carp baked in sour cream................... 70

Canadian trout.................................... 70

CHAPTER 19 DINNER: Variety of steaks: from fish to game... 71

Ribeye steak with cheese sauce........... 71

New York strip steak with shrimp butter 71

Pork steak with mustard cream sauce...72

Sirloin steak with pepper sauce.............72

Flat iron steak with meat sauce............73

Tuna steak glazed with caviar sauce.....73

CHAPTER 20 DINNER: Festive recipes for carnivores: feel comfortable at all times...... 74

Steak and kidney pie (Carnivore Diet Version)... 74

Turkey baked whole (Carnivore Diet Version)... 74

Baked beef with rosemary oil (Carnivore Diet Version).......................................75

Butter braised grouse, capon, or teal duck (Carnivore Diet Version)...................... 75

BBQ Pork ribs (Carnivore Diet Version) 76

Carnivore-friendly beef Wellington (Carnivore Diet Version).......................76

CHAPTER 21: BONUSES.............................77

Meal Plans and Shopping Templates: Streamlined Tools for Easy Keto Meal Planning.................................... 77

    Grocery Shopping List for 7-Day Meal Plan..................................... 77

    Grocery Shopping List for 8-14 Day Meal Plan.................................... 78

    Grocery Shopping List for 15-21 Day Meal Plan..................................79

    Grocery Shopping List for 22-28 Day Meal Plan..................................80

INTRODUCTION

Dear readers,

Emory Stout, a renowned chef and expert in the realm of nutritious cooking, has carved a niche for himself in the art of crafting Carnivore Diet recipes. His dedication to this unique culinary approach, paired with his deep understanding of its health benefits, positions Emory as a leading authority in the field of health-centric gastronomy.

Emory's recipes are a harmonious blend of rich flavors, thoughtfully designed to promote well-being while ensuring each meal is both satisfying and delicious. He embodies the philosophy of enjoying food while maintaining a health-conscious diet, and his passion is evident in every culinary creation he offers.

His journey in mastering the Carnivore Diet is fueled by a combination of personal experience and professional expertise. Acknowledging the challenges and nuances of adopting this lifestyle, Emory leverages his own transformative culinary experiences to inspire and guide others on their paths to wellness.

With his book Emory aims to redefine how we approach health and nutrition. This all-encompassing guide is tailored to help readers achieve their health objectives through a structured 30-day meal plan focused on weight loss, boosted energy levels, enhanced mental clarity, reduced inflammation, and balanced blood sugar.

Under Emory Stout's guidance, embarking on the Carnivore Diet is not just attainable but an exciting journey filled with vibrant flavors and the promise of robust health.

CHAPTER 1: UNDERSTANDING THE STRICT CARNIVORE DIET

The Basics of the Carnivore Diet: What You Need to Know

The Carnivore Diet is a unique nutritional approach that focuses exclusively on animal-based foods, eliminating all plant-based foods, including fruits, vegetables, grains, nuts, and seeds. This diet is rooted in the belief that humans thrive on a diet that is rich in animal fats and proteins, mirroring what our ancestors likely consumed.

What Is the Carnivore Diet?

At its core, the Carnivore Diet is about simplicity and focusing on nutrient-dense, animal-based foods. The diet primarily consists of:

Meat: Beef, pork, lamb, and poultry are staples. Organ meats like liver and kidneys are highly recommended for their dense nutrient profile.

Fish and Seafood: Fatty fish like salmon, mackerel, and sardines, along with shellfish, provide essential omega-3 fatty acids.

Eggs: A great source of protein and healthy fats.

Dairy: While not mandatory, some people include full-fat dairy like butter, cheese, and cream, as long as they can tolerate it.

Animal Fats: Tallow, lard, and bone marrow are used for cooking and as dietary fats.

Why Choose the Carnivore Diet?

The Carnivore Diet is praised for several potential health benefits, especially for those struggling with chronic health issues, including:

Weight Loss: The diet's high protein and fat content promotes satiety, helping to reduce calorie intake naturally. It also stabilizes blood sugar levels, making it easier to manage weight.

Reduced Inflammation: By eliminating plant-based foods that can sometimes trigger inflammation or autoimmune responses, many individuals experience significant reductions in chronic inflammation.

Improved Mental Clarity and Energy Levels: Without the blood sugar spikes and crashes associated with carb-heavy diets, many report sustained energy and sharper mental focus throughout the day.

Simplified Eating: With fewer food choices, meal planning becomes straightforward, which can reduce stress around food decisions and dietary compliance.

Understanding Nutritional Needs

While the Carnivore Diet eliminates many traditional sources of vitamins and minerals, it compensates through nutrient-dense animal products. For example:

Vitamin B12: Found in abundance in red meat and organ meats, B12 is crucial for energy production and neurological function.

Iron: Heme iron, found in meat, is easily absorbed by the body and supports oxygen transport in the blood.

Omega-3 Fatty Acids: Essential for heart and brain health, these are found in fatty fish and grass-fed meats.

Collagen: Found in connective tissues and bones, collagen supports joint health, skin elasticity, and gut health.

Getting Started

Starting the Carnivore Diet involves transitioning from a carbohydrate-based diet to one that relies solely on animal products. It's recommended to:

Start with the Basics: Focus on high-quality meats, and gradually incorporate organ meats and other animal products.

Listen to Your Body: Pay attention to how your body responds, and make adjustments as needed. Some may experience an adaptation period where energy levels fluctuate as the body switches from burning carbs to fats.

Stay Hydrated: Ensure you drink plenty of water and consider supplementing with electrolytes to maintain balance, especially in the early stages of the diet.

Conclusion

The Carnivore Diet is more than just a dietary choice—it's a lifestyle that can lead to significant health improvements when approached with the right mindset and information. Whether you're looking to lose weight, reduce inflammation, or simply explore a new way of eating, the Carnivore Diet offers a unique and effective approach to health and wellness.

Nutritional Benefits of a Meat-Only Diet

The Carnivore Diet, which emphasizes the consumption of meat and animal products while excluding plant-based foods, offers a unique nutritional profile that supports various aspects of health and wellness. Let's explore the key nutritional benefits of a meat-only diet.

High-Quality Protein

One of the most significant benefits of a meat-only diet is its rich source of high-quality protein. Animal proteins contain all nine essential amino acids, which are vital for muscle growth, repair, and overall bodily function. Unlike plant-based proteins, animal proteins are more bioavailable, meaning the body can absorb and utilize them more efficiently.

Rich in Essential Vitamins and Minerals

A meat-only diet provides a concentrated source of essential vitamins and minerals, many of which are more readily absorbed in their animal-derived form:

Vitamin B12: Found exclusively in animal products, Vitamin B12 is crucial for nerve function, DNA synthesis, and red blood cell formation. It's a common deficiency in plant-based diets but is abundantly available in meat, particularly in organ meats like liver.

Iron: Meat, especially red meat, is rich in heme iron, the most absorbable form of iron. Iron is essential for oxygen transport in the blood and supports immune function and cognitive health.

Zinc: Essential for immune function, wound healing, and DNA synthesis, zinc is highly concentrated in meats like beef and lamb.

Vitamin D: Fatty fish, liver, and egg yolks are excellent sources of Vitamin D, which supports bone health, immune function, and mood regulation.

Omega-3 Fatty Acids: Found in fatty fish like salmon and sardines, omega-3s are crucial for heart health, reducing inflammation, and supporting brain function.

Healthy Fats for Energy and Hormone Balance

The Carnivore Diet is high in healthy fats, which serve as the body's primary energy source in the absence of carbohydrates. These fats, including saturated fats and omega-3 fatty acids, are crucial for hormone production, brain health, and cellular integrity.

- **Saturated Fats:** Found in animal products like beef, butter, and pork, these fats are essential for hormone production and absorption of fat-soluble vitamins (A, D, E, and K).
- **Omega-3 Fatty Acids:** Besides supporting heart health, omega-3s have anti-inflammatory properties and are vital for cognitive function.

Supports Blood Sugar Regulation

Without carbohydrates, the body relies on fats for energy, leading to more stable blood sugar levels and reducing the risk of insulin spikes. This can be particularly beneficial for individuals with insulin resistance or type 2 diabetes. The high protein and fat content of the Carnivore Diet also promotes satiety, reducing hunger and helping to regulate appetite more effectively.

Reduced Inflammation and Improved Immune Function

By eliminating potentially inflammatory foods like grains, sugars, and vegetable oils, the Carnivore Diet can help reduce chronic inflammation. The diet's focus on nutrient-dense meats also provides essential nutrients like zinc and vitamin D, which are critical for a well-functioning immune system.

Enhanced Mental Clarity and Cognitive Function

Many people on the Carnivore Diet report improved mental clarity and focus. This could be due to the steady energy supply from fats and the absence of blood sugar fluctuations. Additionally, the diet's rich supply of omega-3 fatty acids and B vitamins supports brain health and cognitive function.

Conclusion

The nutritional benefits of a meat-only diet are extensive, offering a robust profile of essential nutrients that support overall health, energy levels, mental clarity, and more. While the Carnivore Diet might seem restrictive, it provides an array of health benefits through nutrient-dense, animal-based foods that are essential for maintaining optimal health. Whether you're new to the Carnivore Diet or looking to deepen your understanding, recognizing these nutritional benefits can help you make informed choices about your diet and lifestyle.

Common Myths and Misconceptions about the Carnivore Diet

The Carnivore Diet, which focuses exclusively on consuming animal-based foods, has sparked a lot of debate and curiosity. Along with its rise in popularity, a number of myths and misconceptions have emerged. Let's address some of the most common ones:

Myth 1: The Carnivore Diet Lacks Essential Nutrients

Misconception: Many people believe that a diet consisting only of animal products is nutritionally deficient, particularly in vitamins and minerals typically associated with fruits, vegetables, and grains.

Reality: The Carnivore Diet, when followed correctly, can provide all essential nutrients. Meat, especially organ meats like liver, is rich in vitamins and minerals such as Vitamin B12, iron, zinc, and even Vitamin C in trace amounts. Fatty fish provide omega-3 fatty acids and Vitamin D. While the diet does lack certain plant-based nutrients, proponents argue that these are not essential when the body is well-supplied with animal-derived nutrients.

Myth 2: The Carnivore Diet Causes Heart Disease

Misconception: Due to the high intake of saturated fats and cholesterol from animal products, many assume that the Carnivore Diet increases the risk of heart disease.

Reality: Recent studies have challenged the traditional view that dietary cholesterol and saturated fat are the primary causes of heart disease. Instead, it's becoming clearer that inflammation and oxidative stress, often driven by high carbohydrate intake and processed foods, are more significant contributors. Many on the Carnivore Diet report improved cholesterol profiles and reduced markers of inflammation. However, individual results may vary, and it's important to monitor your health markers regularly.

Myth 3: You'll Suffer from Vitamin C Deficiency

Misconception: Without fruits and vegetables, which are common sources of Vitamin C, people often worry that the Carnivore Diet will lead to scurvy or other health issues related to Vitamin C deficiency.

Reality: While Vitamin C is traditionally associated with plant foods, small amounts are present in raw meat and organs. Moreover, the Carnivore Diet reduces the need for Vitamin C because it eliminates high-carbohydrate foods, which increase the body's requirement for this vitamin. As a result, many who follow this diet do not experience the deficiency symptoms often expected.

Myth 4: The Carnivore Diet is Unbalanced and Unsustainable

Misconception: Critics argue that a diet without plant foods is inherently unbalanced and cannot be sustained over the long term without negative consequences.

Reality: Many people have followed the Carnivore Diet for years with reported success in managing chronic health conditions, achieving stable energy levels, and maintaining overall well-being. The key is understanding your body's needs and adjusting your diet accordingly. While it may seem restrictive, those who thrive on this diet find it highly satisfying and sustainable.

Myth 5: The Carnivore Diet Leads to Constipation and Digestive Issues

Misconception: The absence of fiber, which is traditionally thought to be necessary for digestive health, leads some to believe that the Carnivore Diet will cause constipation and other digestive problems.

Reality: Surprisingly, many people on the Carnivore Diet report improved digestion and fewer digestive issues. The diet's high-fat content provides lubrication for the digestive tract, and many find that their bowel movements become more regular. However, individual responses can vary, and staying hydrated and consuming enough fat can help alleviate any digestive discomfort.

Conclusion

The Carnivore Diet, like any dietary approach, is surrounded by myths and misconceptions. While it challenges conventional dietary wisdom, many of these concerns can be addressed with a deeper understanding of how the diet works. As with any significant lifestyle change, it's essential to listen to your body, monitor your health markers, and consult with a healthcare professional, especially if you have pre-existing conditions. By dispelling these myths, you can make a more informed decision about whether the Carnivore Diet is right for you.

Key Components: The Staples of a Carnivore Diet

Understanding the key components of this diet is essential for those who want to embrace its principles fully.

1. Red Meat

Red meat, including beef, lamb, and pork, forms the foundation of the Carnivore Diet. These meats are rich in high-quality protein, essential fatty acids, iron, zinc, and B vitamins, particularly B12. They are also a source of creatine and carnosine, compounds that support muscle function and cognitive health.

- **Beef:** Ground beef, steaks, roasts, and organ meats like liver are staples. Grass-fed options are often preferred for their slightly higher omega-3 content.
- **Lamb:** Known for its rich flavor and high iron content, lamb is another excellent choice.
- **Pork:** Bacon, pork chops, and pork belly are popular for their versatility and fat content.

2. Poultry

Poultry, including chicken, turkey, and duck, offers a leaner protein source while still providing essential nutrients.

- **Chicken:** Whole chickens, thighs, breasts, and wings are common, often cooked with the skin on to retain fat content.
- **Turkey:** Like chicken, turkey is valued for its lean protein but also includes fattier cuts like thighs and drumsticks.

- **Duck:** Known for its rich, flavorful meat, duck is higher in fat, making it a popular choice among carnivore dieters.

3. Fish and Seafood

Fish and seafood are integral to the Carnivore Diet, providing omega-3 fatty acids, iodine, selenium, and a variety of vitamins.

- **Fatty Fish:** Salmon, mackerel, and sardines are high in omega-3 fatty acids, supporting heart health and reducing inflammation.
- **Shellfish:** Shrimp, crab, lobster, and oysters are nutrient-dense, offering a range of minerals and vitamins, including zinc and Vitamin B12.

4. Eggs

Eggs are a versatile and nutrient-packed staple, providing high-quality protein, healthy fats, and essential nutrients like choline and Vitamin D.

- **Whole Eggs:** Typically consumed in various forms, from boiled to scrambled, eggs are an easy addition to any meal.
- **Duck and Quail Eggs:** These are sometimes used for variety, offering slightly different nutritional profiles.

5. Dairy (Optional)

While some on the Carnivore Diet choose to avoid dairy, it can be included depending on individual tolerance.

- **Cheese:** Hard and aged cheeses like cheddar, gouda, and parmesan are popular for their fat content and flavor.
- **Butter and Ghee:** These are used for cooking and adding fat to meals, providing a rich source of conjugated linoleic acid (CLA) and fat-soluble vitamins.
- **Cream:** Heavy cream is often used in recipes or as an addition to coffee.

6. Organ Meats

Organ meats are a cornerstone of the Carnivore Diet due to their high nutrient density.

- **Liver:** Often considered a superfood, liver is packed with vitamins A, B12, and folate, making it a highly nutritious option.
- **Kidneys, Heart, and Bone Marrow:** These organs provide additional nutrients like iron, zinc, and collagen, supporting overall health.

7. Animal Fats

Fats are an essential part of the Carnivore Diet, providing energy and supporting hormone production.

- **Beef Tallow:** Rendered beef fat used for cooking and adding flavor to dishes.
- **Lard:** Rendered pork fat, commonly used in cooking and baking.
- **Duck Fat:** Known for its rich flavor, duck fat is often used in frying and roasting.

Conclusion

The Carnivore Diet revolves around these staple foods, focusing on high-quality, nutrient-dense animal products. By incorporating a variety of meats, fish, eggs, and optional dairy, followers can ensure they meet their nutritional needs while enjoying a diverse and satisfying diet.

The Role of Fat and Protein: Balancing Your Macros

In the Carnivore Diet, understanding the role of fat and protein is crucial to achieving optimal health and maintaining energy levels. Unlike traditional diets that balance carbohydrates, fats, and proteins, the Carnivore Diet focuses almost exclusively on animal-based foods, emphasizing fat and protein as the primary macronutrients.

Protein: The Building Block of Life

Protein is essential for muscle repair, hormone production, and overall body function. On a Carnivore Diet, protein primarily comes from meat, fish, eggs, and dairy, if tolerated.

- **Muscle Maintenance and Growth:** High-quality protein sources like beef, chicken, and fish provide all the essential amino acids your body needs to build and repair muscle tissues. This is particularly important if you're active or aiming to increase muscle mass.
- **Satiety and Weight Management:** Protein is highly satiating, meaning it keeps you feeling full longer, which can help with weight management. Consuming adequate protein helps prevent overeating and supports metabolic function.

Fat: Your Primary Fuel Source

Fat plays a dual role in the Carnivore Diet: it acts as a primary energy source and supports vital bodily functions.

- **Energy Production:** With the absence of carbohydrates, your body shifts to using fat as its main energy source. This metabolic state, known as ketosis, enables your body to burn fat efficiently, leading to weight loss and sustained energy levels throughout the day.
- **Hormone Balance:** Dietary fats are crucial for the production of hormones, including testosterone and estrogen. Consuming enough fat ensures that your endocrine system functions properly, supporting overall health and well-being.
- **Nutrient Absorption:** Fats aid in the absorption of fat-soluble vitamins (A, D, E, and K), which are vital for immune function, bone health, and cellular protection.

Balancing Your Macros: How to Get It Right

Finding the right balance of fat and protein is essential on the Carnivore Diet, and it can vary based on individual goals and needs.

- **Typical Ratios:** A common approach is to aim for a macronutrient ratio where fat constitutes about 65-80% of total daily calories, and protein makes up 20-35%. This ratio helps ensure you're getting enough energy from fat while consuming sufficient protein for muscle maintenance.
- **Listening to Your Body:** It's important to adjust your intake based on how your body responds. Some individuals may thrive on higher fat intake, while others may need more protein to feel satisfied and maintain muscle mass.

Practical Tips for Balancing Macros

- **Choose Fatty Cuts of Meat:** Opt for cuts like ribeye steak, pork belly, and lamb shoulder, which naturally have a higher fat content.

- **Incorporate Organ Meats:** Liver, heart, and kidneys are not only nutrient-dense but also rich in fats and essential vitamins.
- **Use Cooking Fats:** Cook with butter, ghee, tallow, or lard to increase your fat intake, enhancing both flavor and nutrition.

Conclusion

Balancing fat and protein on the Carnivore Diet is key to optimizing health, sustaining energy, and achieving your dietary goals. By prioritizing high-quality animal-based foods and paying attention to your body's needs, you can find the right macro balance that works for you. Whether your goal is weight loss, muscle gain, or overall well-being, understanding the role of these macronutrients will set you on the path to success.

Harnessing Nutrients for Optimal Health on the Carnivore Diet

While this diet doesn't focus on strict macronutrient ratios or calorie counting, understanding the general nutritional intake is beneficial, especially for those transitioning to this lifestyle.

Caloric Intake

Daily caloric needs vary depending on factors like age, gender, activity level, and metabolic goals. Typically:

- **Men**: 2,500 to 3,000 kcal
- **Women**: 2,000 to 2,400 kcal

Since the diet is rich in proteins and fats, it naturally regulates appetite and energy intake allowing most people to eat to satiety without over-consuming calories.

Macronutrient Breakdown

- **Fats**: Constituting 60-80% of your daily energy intake, fats are the primary energy source on the Carnivore Diet. Focus on fattier cuts of meat to ensure adequate energy intake throughout the day.
- **Proteins**: Making up 20-30% of your daily calories, protein intake is crucial for muscle maintenance and overall bodily functions. For example, a person weighing 70 kg might consume 100-140 grams of protein per day, depending on activity level and goals.
- **Carbohydrates**: Carbs are minimal on this diet, typically less than 10 grams per day, primarily coming from dairy products if included.

Micronutrient Considerations

Despite the diet's focus on animal products, it's essential to ensure adequate intake of vitamins and minerals. Here are key nutrients and their sources:

Vitamin A:

Men: 900 mcg
Women: 700 mcg

B Vitamins:

Vitamin B1 (Thiamine): Men — 1.2 mg Women — 1.1 mg
Vitamin B2 (Riboflavin): Men — 1.3 mg Women — 1.1 mg
Vitamin B3 (Niacin): Men — 16 mg NE Women — 14 mg NE

Vitamin B5 (Pantothenic Acid): 5 mg for adults
Vitamin B6 (Pyridoxine): Men — 1.3-1.7 mg;
Women — 1.3-1.5 mg
Vitamin B7 (Biotin): 30 mcg for adults
Vitamin B9 (Folate): 400 mcg for adults
Vitamin B12 (Cobalamin): 2.4 mcg for adults

Iron:

Men: 8 mg
Women: 18 mg (for premenopausal women, 8 mg for postmenopausal women)

Zinc:

Men: 11 mg
Women: 8 mg

Balancing Nutrients

On the Carnivore Diet, nutrient intake often happens naturally when consuming a variety of animal products, especially organ meats. However, it's essential to listen to your body and adjust your diet based on how you feel and your health goals.

For example:

- **Include organ meats**: To ensure you're getting enough vitamins like A, D, E, and K, as well as B vitamins.
- **Prioritize fatty cuts of meat**: These provide both energy and fat-soluble vitamins.
- **Consider supplements if needed**: While most nutrients are readily available from a well-rounded carnivore diet, some individuals may benefit from supplements, particularly if they have specific health concerns or dietary restrictions.

Sodium and Electrolytes

With low carbohydrate intake, the body's sodium needs can increase, particularly if you're in ketosis. It's important to monitor your sodium intake and adjust it based on your body's needs, potentially increasing it to maintain electrolyte balance.

Conclusion

Optimizing nutrient intake on the Carnivore Diet is about focusing on high-quality animal foods and ensuring a variety of meats and organ meats in your diet. While this diet naturally provides many essential nutrients, being mindful of your intake helps ensure you're meeting your body's needs for both macro and micronutrients, supporting overall health and well-being.

Guideline for Nutrient Intake on the Carnivore Diet

Nutrient	Recommended Daily Intake for Men	Recommended Daily Intake for Women
Calories	2,500 – 3,000 kcal per day	2,000 – 2,400 kcal per day
Sugars	Negligible to minimal	Negligible to minimal
Fats	60% – 80% of total calorie intake	60% – 80% of total calorie intake
Carbohydrates	Typically less than 5 g per day	Typically less than 5 g per day
Proteins	About 20% – 30% of total calorie intake	About 20% – 30% of total calorie intake
Fiber	0 g	0 g
Sodium	Adjust based on individual electrolyte needs, particularly in ketosis	Adjust based on individual electrolyte needs, particularly in ketosis

These values provide a general guideline to help you tailor your Carnivore Diet to your personal health goals, emphasizing a high-fat, moderate-protein, and extremely low-carbohydrate approach.

Key Nutrient Intake and Sources on a Carnivore Diet

Nutrient	Recommended Daily Intake for Men	Recommended Daily Intake for Women	Carnivore Diet Sources
Vitamin A	900 mcg	700 mcg	Beef liver, cod liver
Vitamin B1 (Thiamine)	1.2 mg	1.1 mg	Pork, beef, liver
Vitamin B2 (Riboflavin)	1.3 mg	1.1 mg	Liver, eggs, meat
Vitamin B3 (Niacin)	16 mg NE	14 mg NE	Tuna, beef liver, chicken
Vitamin B5 (Pantothenic Acid)	5 mg	5 mg	Liver, beef, chicken
Vitamin B6 (Pyridoxine)	1.3-1.7 mg	1.3-1.5 mg	Turkey, beef, tuna
Vitamin B7 (Biotin)	30 mcg	30 mcg	Eggs, liver, salmon
Vitamin B9 (Folate)	400 mcg	400 mcg	Beef liver, eggs
Vitamin B12 (Cobalamin)	2.4 mcg	2.4 mcg	Meat, fish, shellfish, liver
Iron	8 mg	18 mg / 8 mg	Beef liver, oysters, beef
Zinc	11 mg	8 mg	Meat, shellfish, cheese

The above food items are key sources of essential nutrients within the carnivore diet. The quantity of these foods required to meet daily intake recommendations varies based on the specific food and how it's prepared. Consulting a healthcare professional for personalized dietary advice is always recommended.

CHAPTER 2: 30-DAY MEAL PLAN

Day	Breakfast (625 kcal)	Lunch (875 kcal)	Snack (375 kcal)	Dinner (625 kcal)
Day 1	Supreme Bacon and Eggs - p.21	Seafood Chowder - p.35	Beef Tartare with Cheese - p.49	Ribeye Steak with Cheese Sauce - p.71
Day 2	Cottage Cheese Mousse - p.26	Stuffed Pork Zrazy - p.39	Chicken Julienne - p.50	Osso Buco Lamb Shank - p.65
Day 3	Ham and Cheese Omelet - p.29	Beef Stroganoff - p.42	Pork Chop Salad with Hard Cheese and Bacon - p.54	Seared Sea Bass with Butter and Cheese Sauce - p.69
Day 4	Cheese and Beef Muffins - p.24	Chicken Thighs with Creamy Sauce - p.45	Deep-Fried Pork - p.51	Beef Chops with Peppercorn Sauce - p.66
Day 5	Soft Baked Eggs - p.25	Creamy Chicken Liver Soup - p.35	Cheese Balls with Slices of Boiled Ham - p.52	Herb-Crusted Rack of Lamb - p.65
Day 6	Quail Eggs in Butter with Beef - p.23	Pork and Lamb Kebab with Sauce - p.41	Meat Boats with Eggs - p.50	Tuna Steak Glazed with Caviar Sauce - p.73
Day 7	Haddock and Egg Fritters - p.32	Butter-Stuffed Beef Cutlet - p.43	Pork Bone Broth with Meatballs - p.57	BBQ Pork Ribs - p.76
Day 8	Salty Cheesecakes with Butter - p.25	Baked Beef in Yogurt - p.43	Egg and Cheese Tacos with Meat Filling - p.52	Wild Salmon Wellington - p.69
Day 9	Chicken Fillet and Feta Cheese Omelet - p.29	Pork Roll with Chicken and Cheese - p.41	Salmon Tartare with Egg Sauce - p.49	Chopped Chicken Cutlets - p.66
Day 10	Meatloaf with Cheese Sauce - p.33	Classic Roast Beef - p.42	Steak and Egg Salad - p.53	Butter-Braised Grouse - p.75
Day 11	Pork Belly Breakfast - p.22	Pork Stew - p.40	Cheese Salad - p.55	Sirloin Steak with Pepper Sauce - p.72
Day 12	Fish Fingers in Egg Batter with Sauce - p.24	Chicken Fricassee - p.46	Beef Bone Broth - p.56	Herb-Crusted Rack of Lamb - p.65
Day 13	Cheese Pancakes with Boiled Egg Circles - p.33	Fish Stew in Clay Pot - p.37	Steak and Egg Salad - p.53	Flat Iron Steak with Meat Sauce - p.73
Day 14	Fried Mini Beef Rolls - p.22	Pepper-Crusted Beef Medallions - p.44	Carnivore Shurpa without Vegetables - p.57	Seared Sea Bass with Butter and Cheese Sauce - p.69
Day 15	Chicken Fillet with Raw Smoked Sausage - p.28	Cream Soup of Beef and Cheese - p.36	Bacon-Wrapped Shrimp Skewers - p.51	Baked Salmon with Herb Crust - p.70
Day 16	Bacon Egg Muffins - p.32	Lamb Ragu Italian-Style - p.38	Pork Lard Chimichurri - p.60	Grilled Beef Tacos on Egg Pancakes - p.68
Day 17	Turkey Tubes with Bacon - p.34	Cream Pork Chops - p.39	Meat Boats with Eggs - p.50	Ribeye Steak with Cheese Sauce - p.71
Day 18	Fried Egg-Breaded Chicken Fillet - p.27	Chicken Thighs with Creamy Sauce - p.45	Chicken Bone Broth with Egg and Chicken Breast - p.56	Pork Steak with Mustard Cream Sauce - p.72
Day 19	Cheese and Egg Burrito with Steak and Bacon - p.23	Braised Beef Tongue - p.38	Cheese Balls with Slices of Boiled Ham - p.52	Steak and Kidney Pie (Carnivore Diet Version) - p.74
Day 20	Cottage Cheese Casserole with Cream - p.62	Stuffed Turkey Patties - p.47	Cheese Salad - p.55	Tuna Steak Glazed with Caviar Sauce - p.73

Day	Breakfast (625 kcal)	Lunch (875 kcal)	Snack (375 kcal)	Dinner (625 kcal)
Day 21	Meat Soufflé - p.28	Chicken Pudding - p.48	Chicken Liver Pâté - p.58	Pork Steak with Mustard Cream Sauce - p.72
Day 22	Beef Forshmak - p.26	Stuffed Pork Zrazy - p.39	Hollandaise Sauce - p.59	Seared Sea Bass with Butter and Cheese Sauce - p.69
Day 23	Quail Eggs with Carpaccio from Smoked Wild Salmon - p.27	Braised Pork Knuckle - p.67	Cheese Salad - p.55	Baked Beef with Rosemary Oil (Carnivore Diet Version) - p.75
Day 24	Salty Cheesecakes with Butter - p.25	Crispy Chicken Tabaka - p.45	Deep-Fried Pork - p.51	Wild Salmon Wellington - p.69
Day 25	Turkey and Cheddar Casserole - p.31	Baked Beef in Yogurt - p.43	Chicken Bone Broth with Egg and Chicken Breast - p.56	Grilled Beef Tacos on Egg Pancakes - p.68
Day 26	Cheese Pancakes with Boiled Egg Circles - p.33	Pork Roll with Chicken and Cheese - p.41	Bacon-Wrapped Shrimp Skewers - p.51	Ribeye Steak with Cheese Sauce - p.71
Day 27	Fish Fingers in Egg Batter with Sauce - p.24	Chicken Fricassee - p.46	Cheese Balls with Slices of Boiled Ham - p.52	Tuna Steak Glazed with Caviar Sauce - p.73
Day 28	Soft Baked Eggs - p.25	Braised Beef Tongue - p.38	Meat Boats with Eggs - p.50	BBQ Pork Ribs (Carnivore Diet Version) - p.76
Day 29	Pork Clipping Stuffed with Cheese - p.21	Pork Stew - p.40	Salmon Tartare with Egg Sauce - p.49	Baked Salmon with Herb Crust (Carnivore Diet Version) - p.70
Day 30	Cheese Soufflé with Bacon - p.34	Stuffed Turkey Patties - p.47	Chicken Liver Pâté - p.58	Pork Chop with Crispy Pork Belly Crust - p.64

Note: This 30-day meal plan is designed with a daily intake of 2,500 calories, spread evenly across four meals. The calorie distribution is designed to ensure that each meal is both nourishing and balanced, providing the necessary energy and nutrients throughout the day.

Breakfast: Start your day with 25% of your daily caloric intake, which equates to approximately 625 calories. This meal might include protein-rich options like a hearty steak or eggs paired with bacon, delivering a solid mix of proteins and fats to fuel your morning.

Lunch: As the most substantial meal of the day, lunch accounts for 35% of your daily calories, totaling around 875 calories. A generous portion of meat such as roast beef or beef ribs could be the main feature, possibly enhanced with added fats like a pat of butter to boost satiety.

Snack: A light yet satisfying snack should make up 15% of your daily intake, around 375 calories. Opt for a small portion of fatty meat or a few slices of cheese if dairy is included in your diet, providing a quick energy boost.

Dinner: Conclude your day with another 25% of your caloric intake, which also amounts to 625 calories. This meal can include a variety of proteins such as fish or chicken, perhaps accompanied by a flavorful animal fat sauce to enrich the dish.

These meal proportions are flexible and can be tailored to fit individual needs and preferences. It's essential to pay attention to your body's cues and adjust portion sizes and nutrient ratios to maintain optimal well-being.

Important Note: Any greens or carbohydrate-rich foods shown in the accompanying photos are intended solely for decorative and aesthetic purposes. Please refer to the recipes for the appropriate ingredients to use in your meal preparation.

CHAPTER 3: BREAKFASTS: Classic carnivore breakfasts

Supreme bacon and eggs

Prep: 5 minutes | Cook: 10 minutes | Serves: 1

Ingredients:

- 6 slices bacon (170g)
- 2 large eggs (100g)
- Salt to taste

Instructions:

1. Cook bacon in a skillet over medium heat until crispy, about 4-5 minutes per side. Remove and set aside.
2. In the same skillet, fry the eggs in the bacon fat to your desired doneness, about 2-3 minutes.
3. Season the eggs with salt and pepper.
4. Serve the crispy bacon alongside the fried eggs.

Nutritional Facts (Per Serving): Calories: 625 | Sugars: 0g | Fat: 45g | Carbs: 0g | Protein: 42g | Fiber: 0g | Sodium: 2000mg | Vitamin A: 300µg | Vitamin B1: 0.3mg | Vitamin B2: 0.5mg | Vitamin B3: 12mg | Vitamin B5: 0mg | Vitamin B6: 0.6mg | Vitamin B7: 0µg | Vitamin B9: 0µg | Vitamin B12: 3.5µg | Iron: 2.5mg | Zinc: 3.5mg

Pork clipping stuffed with cheese

Prep: 10 minutes | Cook: 20 minutes | Serves: 1

Ingredients:

- 1 1/2 cup ground pork (200g)
- 2 oz hard fermented cheese Parmesan (56g)
- 2 quail eggs (50g)
- 2 slices bacon (60g)
- Salt to taste

Instructions:

1. Preheat the oven to 375°F (190°C).
2. Whisk the mincemeat until airy. Form 2 flat patties. Make a slit inside, in each to make a pocket, and fill with cheese. Wrap each cutlet with a slice of bacon and secure with toothpicks.
3. Place the cutlets in a baking dish and bake for 20 minutes, until the pork is cooked through and the bacon is crispy.
4. Serve with the baking juices as a sauce and eggs.

Nutritional Facts (Per Serving): Calories: 625 | Sugars: 0g | Fat: 48g | Carbs: 0g | Protein: 38g | Fiber: 0g | Sodium: 2200mg | Vitamin A: 250µg | Vitamin B1: 0.4mg | Vitamin B2: 0.5mg | Vitamin B3: 15mg | Vitamin B5: 1.8mg | Vitamin B6: 0.5mg | Vitamin B7: 0µg | Vitamin B9: 18µg | Vitamin B12: 2.8µg | Iron: 3mg | Zinc: 4mg

Fried mini beef rolls

Prep: 15 minutes | Cook: 20 minutes | Serves: 1

Ingredients:

- 4 oz ground chicken (113g)
- 1 large egg (50g)
- 4 thin beef slices (200g)
- Salt to taste
- Cooking fat for frying

Instructions:

1. Mix ground chicken with egg, season with salt .
2. Place a spoonful of chicken mixture on each beef slice, roll up and secure with toothpicks.
3. Heat cooking fat in a skillet over medium heat, fry beef rolls until cooked through, about 5-7 minutes per side.
4. Serve with the gravy made from the frying fat.

Nutritional Facts (Per Serving): Calories: 625 | Sugars: 0g | Fat: 42g | Carbs: 0g | Protein: 50g | Fiber: 0g | Sodium: 1600mg | Vitamin A: 200µg | Vitamin B1: 0.3mg | Vitamin B2: 0.6mg | Vitamin B3: 18mg | Vitamin B5: 2mg | Vitamin B6: 0.7mg | Vitamin B7: 0µg | Vitamin B9: 22µg | Vitamin B12: 3µg | Iron: 4.5mg | Zinc: 6mg

Pork belly breakfast

Prep: 10 minutes | Cook: 30 minutes | Serves: 1

Ingredients:

- 8 oz pork belly (227g)
- Salt to taste

Instructions:

1. Preheat the oven to 400 °F (200 °C).
2. Season pork belly with salt, place on a bakin sheet.
3. Roast for 30 minutes until crispy, turning halfway

Nutritional Facts (Per Serving): Calories: 625 | Sugars 0g | Fat: 52g | Carbs: 0g | Protein: 32g | Fiber: 0g Sodium: 1800mg | Vitamin A: 280µg | Vitamin B1: 0.4m | Vitamin B2: 0.5mg | Vitamin B3: 14mg | Vitamin B5 2mg | Vitamin B6: 0.5mg | Vitamin B7: 0µg | Vitamin B9 20µg | Vitamin B12: 3µg | Iron: 2.5mg | Zinc: 3.5mg

Quail eggs in butter with beef

Prep: 10 minutes | Cook: 15 minutes | Serves: 1

Ingredients:

- 4 oz quail eggs (113g)
- 2 oz beef, sliced (57g)
- 2 tbsp butter (28g)
- Salt to taste

Instructions:

1. Melt the butter in a pan over medium heat.
2. Add the sliced beef and cook until browned.
3. Push the beef to one side of the pan and add the quail eggs.
4. Fry the eggs until the whites are set but the yolks are still runny.
5. Season with salt to taste and serve drizzled with melted butter from the pan.

Nutritional Facts (Per Serving): Calories: 625 | Sugars: 0g | Fat: 44g | Carbs: 0g | Protein: 48g | Fiber: 0g | Sodium: 2000mg | Vitamin A: 300µg | Vitamin B1: 0.3mg | Vitamin B2: 0.6mg | Vitamin B3: 15mg | Vitamin B5: 2.2mg | Vitamin B6: 0.7mg | Vitamin B7: 0µg | Vitamin B9: 20µg | Vitamin B12: 3.5µg | Iron: 3mg | Zinc: 4mg

Cheese and egg burrito with steak and bacon

Prep: 10 minutes | Cook: 15 minutes | Serves: 1

Ingredients:

- 3 oz ribeye steak (85g)
- 2 slices bacon (30g)
- 2 large eggs (100g)
- 2 oz cheddar cheese, shredded (55g)
- Salt taste

Instructions:

1. Cook the bacon in a skillet over medium heat until crispy. Remove and set aside.
2. In the same skillet, cook the ribeye steak to your desired doneness, seasoning with salt and pepper. Remove and slice thinly.
3. Beat the eggs and cook them in the skillet until scrambled.
4. Layer the scrambled eggs, steak slices, and shredded cheddar cheese on the cooked bacon slices. Roll them up to form a burrito.
5. Serve immediately.

Nutritional Facts (Per Serving): Calories: 625 | Sugars: 0g | Fat: 46g | Carbs: 0g | Protein: 45g | Fiber: 0g | Sodium: 2100mg | Vitamin A: 250µg | Vitamin B1: 0.4mg | Vitamin B2: 0.6mg | Vitamin B3: 14mg | Vitamin B5: 2mg | Vitamin B6: 0.6mg | Vitamin B7: 0µg | Vitamin B9: 20µg | Vitamin B12: 3µg | Iron: 3mg | Zinc: 4.5mg

Fish fingers in egg batter with sauce

Prep: 10 minutes | Cook: 15 minutes | Serves: 1

Ingredients:

- 4 oz halibut fillets, cut into fingers (113g)
- 1 large egg (50g)
- 2 tbsp beef tallow (28g)
- 2 tbsp butter (28g)l
- Salt to taste

Instructions:

1. Beat the egg in a shallow bowl and season with salt.
2. Dip the halibut fingers into the egg to coat.
3. Heat the beef tallow in a pan over medium-high heat.
4. Fry the fish fingers until golden brown and cooked through, about 2-3 minutes per side.
5. Serve the fish with any remaining fat from the pan for a richer flavor.

Nutritional Facts (Per Serving): Calories: 625 | Sugars: 0g | Fat: 45g | Carbs: 0g | Protein: 42g | Fiber: 0g | Sodium: 2000mg | Vitamin A: 300µg | Vitamin B1: 0.4mg | Vitamin B2: 0.8mg | Vitamin B3: 16mg | Vitamin B5: 2.4mg | Vitamin B6: 0.6mg | Vitamin B7: 27µg | Vitamin B9: 60µg | Vitamin B12: 4.3µg | Iron: 3.6mg | Zinc: 4mg

Cheese and beef muffins

Prep: 10 minutes | Cook: 15 minutes | Serves: 1

Ingredients:

- 2 oz ground beef (57g)
- 2 oz cheddar cheese, shredded (57g)
- 2 large eggs (100g)
- 1 tbsp butter (14g)
- Salt to taste

Instructions:

1. Preheat the oven to 350°F (180°C).
2. In a pan, cook the ground beef over medium heat until browned.
3. In a bowl, whisk the eggs and season with salt.
4. Mix the ground beef and shredded cheddar cheese into the eggs.
5. Grease a muffin tin with butter and pour the mixture into one cup.
6. Bake for 12-15 minutes, until set.
7.Serve the muffins with any remaining fat from the pan for added richness..

Nutritional Facts (Per Serving): Calories: 625 | Sugars: 0g | Fat: 45g | Carbs: 0g | Protein: 42g | Fiber: 0g | Sodium: 2000mg | Vitamin A: 300µg | Vitamin B1: 0.4mg | Vitamin B2: 0.8mg | Vitamin B3: 16mg | Vitamin B5: 2.4mg | Vitamin B6: 0.6mg | Vitamin B7: 27µg | Vitamin B9: 60µg | Vitamin B12: 4.3µg | Iron: 3.6mg | Zinc: 4mg

CHAPTER 4: BREAKFASTS: Morning fuel: quick and delicious breakfasts

Salty cheesecakes with butter

Prep: 15 minutes | Cook: 20 minutes | Serves: 1

Ingredients:

- 8 oz cottage cheese (225g)
- 2 large eggs (120g)
- 2 tbsp butter (30g)
- 4 slices bacon (120g)
- Salt to taste

Instructions:

1. Preheat the oven to 375°F (190°C). In a bowl, mix the cottage cheese with the eggs and a pinch of salt.

2. Form small cheesecakes and place them on a baking sheet lined with parchment paper. Bake for 15-20 minutes until golden brown.

3. While baking, cook the bacon in a pan until crispy. Reserve the bacon fat. Serve the cheesecakes with a drizzle of melted butter and toasted bacon sauce made from the bacon fat.

Nutritional Facts (Per Serving): Calories: 625 | Sugars: 0g | Fat: 45g | Carbs: 0g | Protein: 42g | Fiber: 0g | Sodium: 2000mg | Vitamin A: 300µg | Vitamin B1: 0.4mg | Vitamin B2: 0.8mg | Vitamin B3: 16mg | Vitamin B5: 2.4mg | Vitamin B6: 0.6mg | Vitamin B7: 27µg | Vitamin B9: 60µg | Vitamin B12: 4.3µg | Iron: 3.6mg | Zinc: 4mg

Soft baked eggs

Prep: 10 minutes | Cook: 15 minutes | Serves: 2

Ingredients:

- 2 large eggs (120g)
- Salt to taste
- 2 tbsp butter (28g), plus more for greasing

Instructions:

1. Preheat the oven to 350°F (175°C).
2. Grease two small ramekins with butter.
3. Crack an egg into each ramekin and season with salt and pepper.
4. Bake in the oven for 12-15 minutes until the whites are set but the yolks are still runny.
5. Serve with a drizzle of melted butter on top for extra richness.

Nutritional Facts (Per Serving): Calories: 625 | Sugars: 0g | Fat: 45g | Carbs: 0g | Protein: 42g | Fiber: 0g | Sodium: 1800mg | Vitamin A: 280µg | Vitamin B1: 0.4mg | Vitamin B2: 0.6mg | Vitamin B3: 14mg | Vitamin B5: 2.4mg | Vitamin B6: 0.6mg | Vitamin B7: 27µg | Vitamin B9: 60µg | Vitamin B12: 4.3µg | Iron: 3.6mg | Zinc: 4mg

Cottage cheese mousse

Prep: 10 minutes | Cook: 15 minutes | Serves: 1

Ingredients:

- 1 cup full-fat cottage cheese (225 g, no additives)
- 2 tbsp. l. ghee or butter (30 g)
- Salt to taste

Instructions:

1. Mix cottage cheese and ghee (or butter) until smooth.
2. Season with a pinch of salt.
3. Serve immediately or chill for 30 minutes for a firmer texture.

Nutritional Facts (Per Serving): Calories: 625 | Sugars: 0g | Fat: 45g | Carbs: 0g | Protein: 42g | Fiber: 0g | Sodium: 2000mg | Vitamin A: 300µg | Vitamin B1: 0.4mg | Vitamin B2: 0.8mg | Vitamin B3: 16mg | Vitamin B5: 2.4mg | Vitamin B6: 0.6mg | Vitamin B7: 27µg | Vitamin B9: 60µg | Vitamin B12: 4.3µg | Iron: 3.6mg | Zinc: 4mg

Beef forshmak

Prep: 15 minutes | Cook: 30 minutes | Serves: 1

Ingredients:

- 8 oz beef loin (225g)
- 2 tbsp heavy cream (30ml)
- 2 tbsp ghee or butter (30 ml)
- Salt to taste

Instructions:

1. Boil the beef loin until tender, about 30 minutes.
2. Mince the boiled beef finely.
3. Mix the minced beef with heavy cream
4. Season with salt.
5. Serve warm.

Nutritional Facts (Per Serving): Calories: 625 | Sugars 0g | Fat: 42g | Carbs: 2g | Protein: 58g | Fiber: 0g Sodium: 300mg | Vitamin A: 500µg | Vitamin B1: 0.1mg Vitamin B2: 0.4mg | Vitamin B3: 5mg | Vitamin B5: 1mg Vitamin B6: 0.5mg | Vitamin B7: 10µg | Vitamin B9: 20µ | Vitamin B12: 4µg | Iron: 4mg | Zinc: 7mg

Fried egg-breaded chicken fillet

Prep: 10 minutes | Cook: 25 minutes | Serves: 1

Ingredients:

- 1 chicken fillet (200g)
- 2 large eggs (120g)
- Salt to taste
- 2 tbsp butter (30g)

Instructions:

1. Beat the eggs in a bowl with salt .
2. Dip the chicken fillet in the egg mixture, ensuring it's fully coated.
3. Melt the butter in a pan over medium heat.
4. Fry the chicken fillet until golden brown and cooked through, about 8-10 minutes per side.
5. Serve hot.

Nutritional Facts (Per Serving): Calories: 625 | Sugars: 1g | Fat: 48g | Carbs: 2g | Protein: 48g | Fiber: 0g | Sodium: 600mg | Vitamin A: 700µg | Vitamin B1: 0.1mg | Vitamin B2: 0.4mg | Vitamin B3: 6mg | Vitamin B5: 1.5mg | Vitamin B6: 0.7mg | Vitamin B7: 10µg | Vitamin B9: 50µg | Vitamin B12: 1.5µg | Iron: 1.5mg | Zinc: 2mg

Quail eggs with carpaccio from salty wild salmon

Prep: 10 minutes | Cook: 15 minutes | Serves: 1

Ingredients:

- 4 quail eggs (50g)
- 3 slices salty wild salmon (85g)
- 2 tbsp butter (30g)
- Salt to taste

Instructions:

1. Hard boil the quail eggs for 4 minutes, then cool and peel.
2. Slice the eggs in half and arrange on a plate with salty salmon.
3.drizzle with butter .
4. Serve immediately.

Nutritional Facts (Per Serving): Calories: 625 | Sugars: 0g | Fat: 50g | Carbs: 1g | Protein: 45g | Fiber: 0g | Sodium: 1200mg | Vitamin A: 900µg | Vitamin B1: 0.1mg | Vitamin B2: 0.5mg | Vitamin B3: 6mg | Vitamin B5: 1.5mg | Vitamin B6: 0.7mg | Vitamin B7: 10µg | Vitamin B9: 50µg | Vitamin B12: 4.5µg | Iron: 2mg | Zinc: 2mg

Chicken fillet with dry-cured sausage

Prep: 15 minutes | Cook: 20 minutes | Serves: 1

Ingredients:

- 1 chicken fillet (200g)
- 3 slices of natural dry-cured sausage without additives (85 g)
- 1/4 cup of grated cheese (30 g) - hard cheese without additives Cheddar
- 1 large egg (60g)
- 2 tbsp butter (30g)

Instructions:

1. Preheat the oven to 375°F (190°C).
2. Pound the chicken fillet to an even thickness.
3. Place the sausage slices on top of the chicken fillet, then sprinkle with cheese.
4. Bake for 15-20 minutes until the chicken is cooked through. Fry the egg in a pan and place it on top of the baked chicken fillet.
5. Serve immediately.

Nutritional Facts (Per Serving): Calories: 625 | Sugars: 1g | Fat: 46g | | Protein: 51g | Fiber: 0g | Sodium: 1100mg | Vitamin A: 700µg | Vitamin B1: 0.1mg | Vitamin B2: 0.4mg | Vitamin B3: 5mg | Vitamin B5: 1.5mg | Vitamin B6: 0.7mg | Vitamin B7: 10µg | Vitamin B9: 50µg | Vitamin B12: 1.5µg | Iron: 1.5mg | Zinc: 2mg

Meat soufflé

Prep: 15 minutes | Cook: 30 minutes | Serves: 1

Ingredients:

- 8 oz ground beef (225g)
- 2 large eggs (120g)
- Salt to taste
- 2 tbsp cream or meat sauce (30 ml)

Instructions:

1. Preheat the oven to 350°F (175°C).
2. In a bowl, mix the ground beef with eggs, salt.
3. Pour the mixture into a greased ramekin.
4. Bake for 25-30 minutes until set and slightly puffed.
5. Serve with cream or meat sauce on top.

Nutritional Facts (Per Serving): Calories: 625 | Sugars: 0g | Fat: 47g | | Protein: 47g | Fiber: 0g | Sodium: 400mg | Vitamin A: 300µg | Vitamin B1: 0.1mg | Vitamin B2: 0.4mg | Vitamin B3: 5mg | Vitamin B5: 1.5mg | Vitamin B6: 0.5mg | Vitamin B7: 10µg | Vitamin B9: 20µg | Vitamin B12: 4µg | Iron: 4mg | Zinc: 7mg

CHAPTER 5: BREAKFASTS: Omelettes and Casseroles

Chicken fillet and cheddar cheese omelet

Prep: 10 minutes | Cook: 15 minutes | Serves: 1

Ingredients:

- 3 large eggs (150g)
- 4 oz chicken fillet, cooked and chopped (115g)
- 2 oz Cheddar cheese, crumbled (55g)
- 1 tbsp butter (15g)
- Salt to taste

Instructions:

. Beat the eggs with salt. Melt the butter in a on-stick pan over medium heat.

. Add the eggs and let them set slightly before dding the chicken and feta cheese.

. Cook until the eggs are fully set and the cheese s melted. Serve hot.

Nutritional Facts (Per Serving): Calories: 625 | Sugars: g | Fat: 47g || Protein: 51g | Fiber: 0g | Sodium: 920 mg Vitamin A: 500µg | Vitamin B1: 0.1mg | Vitamin B2: .6mg | Vitamin B3: 15mg | Vitamin B5: 1.5mg | Vitamin 6: 1.2mg | Vitamin B7: 0µg | Vitamin B9: 70µg | Vitamin 12: 1.8µg | Iron: 3mg | Zinc: 4mg

Ham and cheese omelet

Prep: 10 minutes | Cook: 15 mins | Serves: 1

Ingredients:

- 3 large eggs (150g)
- 3 ounces natural meat (ham or other type without additives, 85 g)
- 2 oz Cheddar cheese, shredded (55g)
- 1 tbsp butter (15g)
- Salt to taste

Instructions:

1. Beat the eggs with salt . Melt the butter in a non-stick pan over medium heat.

2. Add the eggs and let them set slightly before adding the ham and Cheddar cheese.

3. Cook until the eggs are fully set and the cheese is melted. Serve hot.

Nutritional Facts (Per Serving): Calories: 625 | Sugars: 0g | Fat: 48g | | Protein: 47g | Fiber: 0g | Sodium: 1100mg | Vitamin A: 600µg | Vitamin B1: 0.1mg | Vitamin B2: 0.6mg | Vitamin B3: 8mg | Vitamin B5: 1.5mg | Vitamin B6: 0.8mg | Vitamin B7: 0µg | Vitamin B9: 60µg | Vitamin B12: 2.7µg | Iron: 2.5mg | Zinc: 4mg

Fish fingers and egg casserole

Prep: 15 minutes | Cook: 25 minutes | Serves: 1

Ingredients:

- 4 oz haddock, thinly sliced (115g)
- 1 oz lard, cut into strips (30g)
- 3 large eggs (150g)
- 2 tbsp. l. ghee or ghee (30 ml)1/4
- Salt r to taste

Instructions:

1. Preheat the oven to 375°F (190°C).
2. Roll the haddock slices with lard strips and secure with toothpicks.
3. Pan-fry the haddock rolls until golden brown.
4. Separate the whites from the yolks. Whisk the egg whites with salt . Place the haddock rolls in the baking dish and pour the beaten egg yolks over them, gently placing a whole egg yolk on top of each one.
5. Bake for 15 minutes or until the eggs are set.
6. Serve with melted butter or ghee.

Nutritional Facts (Per Serving): Calories: 625 | Sugars: 0g | Fat: 48g | | Protein: 44g | Fiber: 0g | Sodium: 700mg | Vitamin A: 600µg | Vitamin B1: 0.1mg | Vitamin B2: 0.5mg | Vitamin B3: 8mg | Vitamin B5: 1.5mg | Vitamin B6: 0.8mg | Vitamin B7: 0µg | Vitamin B9: 50µg | Vitamin B12: 3µg | Iron: 2mg | Zinc: 3mg

Egg casserole with chicken minced meat

Prep: 15 minutes | Cook: 25 minutes | Serves: 1

Ingredients:

- 6 oz chicken minced meat (170g)
- 3 large eggs (150g)
- 1/2 cup (60 g) grated hard cheese (fermented, no additives)
- 2 tbsp (30 ml) melted ghe
- Salt to taste

Instructions:

1. Preheat the oven to 375°F (190°C).
2. Cook the chicken minced meat in a pan unt browned. Beat the eggs with salt .
3. In a baking dish, combine the cooked mince meat and beaten eggs.
4. Sprinkle with grated cheese and bake for 2 minutes or until the eggs are set.
5. Serve drizzled with melted cheese or ghee.

Nutritional Facts (Per Serving): Calories: 625 | Sugars 0g | Fat: 48g | | Protein: 48g | Fiber: 0g | Sodium: 800m | Vitamin A: 500µg | Vitamin B1: 0.1mg | Vitamin B2 0.6mg | Vitamin B3: 10mg | Vitamin B5: 1.5mg | Vitami B6: 0.9mg | Vitamin B7: 0µg | Vitamin B9: 60µg | Vitami B12: 1.5µg | Iron: 2.5mg | Zinc: 4mg

Chicken fillet in cheese and egg dough

Prep: 15 minutes | Cook: 20 minutes | Serves: 1

Ingredients:

- 1 chicken fillet (200g)
- 2 large eggs (100g)
- 1/2 cup shredded hard cheese (60 g)

- 2 tbsp ghee (30 g) or melted cheese
- Salt to taste

Instructions:

1. Preheat the oven to 375°F (190°C).
2. Beat the eggs and mix with shredded cheese, salt, and pepper.
3. Dip the chicken fillet in the egg and cheese mixture.
4. Place the fillet on a baking sheet and bake for 20 minutes or until cooked through.
5. Serve drizzled with ghee or melted cheese

Nutritional Facts (Per Serving): Calories: 625 | Sugars: 0g | Fat: 48g | Protein: 51 | Fiber: 0g | Sodium: 800mg | Vitamin A: 500µg | Vitamin B1: 0.1mg | Vitamin B2: 0.5mg | Vitamin B3: 10mg | Vitamin B5: 1.5mg | Vitamin B6: 1mg | Vitamin B7: 0µg | Vitamin B9: 60µg | Vitamin B12: 1.5µg | Iron: 2mg | Zinc: 4mg

Turkey and cheddar casserole

Prep: 15 minutes | Cook: 25 minutes | Serves: 1

Ingredients:

- 6 oz turkey breast, diced (170g)
- 3 large eggs (150g)
- 1/2 cup shredded Cheddar cheese (60 g)

- 2 tbsp ghee (30 g) (or cream if using)
- Salt to taste

Instructions:

1. Preheat the oven to 375°F (190°C).
2. Beat the eggs with ghee and a little salt.
3. In a baking dish, combine the diced turkey and beaten eggs.
4. Top with shredded Cheddar cheese.
5. Bake for 20-25 minutes or until the eggs are set and the cheese is melted and bubbly.

Nutritional Facts (Per Serving): Calories: 625 | Sugars: 0g | Fat: 48g | Carbs: 1g | Protein: 45g | Fiber: 0g | Sodium: 800mg | Vitamin A: 600µg | Vitamin B1: 0.1mg | Vitamin B2: 0.6mg | Vitamin B3: 10mg | Vitamin B5: 1.5mg | Vitamin B6: 1mg | Vitamin B7: 0µg | Vitamin B9: 60µg | Vitamin B12: 1.5µg | Iron: 2mg | Zinc: 4mg

CHAPTER 6: BREAKFASTS: Family weekend breakfasts

Haddock and egg fritters

Prep: 10 minutes | Cook: 15 minutes | Serves: 1

Ingredients:

- 1 haddock fillet (7 oz) (200g)
- 2 large eggs (100g)
- 2 tbsp butter (30g)
- Salt to taste

Instructions:

1. Finely chop the haddock fillet and mix with the beaten eggs.
2. Heat butter in a pan over medium heat.
3. Drop spoonfuls of the haddock and egg mixture into the pan and cook until golden brown, about 4-5 minutes per side.
4. Season with salt to taste before serving.

Nutritional Facts (Per Serving): Calories: 625 | Sugars: 0g | Fat: 45g | Carbs: 0g | Protein: 55g | Fiber: 0g | Sodium: 400mg | Vitamin A: 0µg | Vitamin B1: 0.1mg | Vitamin B2: 0.3mg | Vitamin B3: 10mg | Vitamin B5: 1mg | Vitamin B6: 0.8mg | Vitamin B7: 0µg | Vitamin B9: 10µg | Vitamin B12: 5µg | Iron: 2mg | Zinc: 1mg

Bacon egg muffins

Prep: 15 minutes | Cook: 15 minutes | Serves: 1

Ingredients:

- 2 large eggs (100g)
- 2 slices smoked bacon (50g)
- Salt to taste

Instructions:

1. Preheat the oven to 375°F (190°C).
2. Line a muffin tin with bacon slices, forming a cup shape.
3. Crack an egg into each bacon cup.
4. Bake for 15 minutes, or until the eggs are set.
5. Season with salt to taste before serving.

Nutritional Facts (Per Serving): Calories: 625 | Sugars: 0g | Fat: 50g | Carbs: 0g | Protein: 40g | Fiber: 0g | Sodium: 900mg | Vitamin A: 0µg | Vitamin B1: 0.1mg | Vitamin B2: 0.4mg | Vitamin B3: 10mg | Vitamin B5: 1.5mg | Vitamin B6: 0.5mg | Vitamin B7: 0µg | Vitamin B9: 12µg | Vitamin B12: 4µg | Iron: 2mg | Zinc: 3mg

Meatloaf with cheese sauce

Prep 15 minutes | Cook: 45 minutes | Serves: 1

Ingredients:

5 oz ground pork (140g)
5 oz ground beef (140g)
1 egg (50g)
1/2 cup shredded cheese
(60g)
Salt to taste

Cheese sauce:
- 1/2 cup heavy cream
  (120ml)
- 1/2 cup shredded cheese
  (60g)
- Salt to taste

Instructions:

1. Preheat the oven to 350°F (175°C).
2. Mix ground pork, ground beef, and egg in a bowl. Season with salt.
3. Form the mixture into a loaf shape and place in a baking dish. Bake for 45 minutes, or until cooked through.
4. For the cheese sauce, heat heavy cream in a saucepan over medium heat until simmering.
5. Add shredded cheese and stir until melted and smooth. Season with salt.
6. Pour the cheese sauce over the meatloaf before serving.

Nutritional Facts (Per Serving): Calories: 625 | Sugars: 0g | Fat: 50g | Carbs: 0g | Protein: 45g | Fiber: 0g | Sodium: 800mg | Vitamin A: 0µg | Vitamin B1: 0.1mg | Vitamin B2: 0.3mg | Vitamin B3: 12mg | Vitamin B5: 1.5mg | Vitamin B6: 0.7mg | Vitamin B7: 0µg | Vitamin B9: 15µg | Vitamin B12: 3µg | Iron: 3mg | Zinc: 4mg

Cheese pancakes with boiled egg circles

Prep: 10 minutes | Cook: 20 minutes | Serves: 1

Ingredients:

- 1/2 cup shredded cheese
  (60g)
- 1 large egg (50g)
- 2 boiled eggs, halved
  (100g)

- 2 tbsp butter (30g)
- Salt to taste

Instructions:

1. Mix shredded cheese and beaten egg to form a batter.
2. Heat butter in a pan over medium heat.
3. Pour small circles of the batter into the pan and cook until golden brown, about 2-3 minutes per side.
4. Top each pancake with a boiled egg half.
5. Season with salt to taste before serving.

Nutritional Facts (Per Serving): Calories: 625 | Sugars: 0g | Fat: 50g | Carbs: 0g | Protein: 45g | Fiber: 0g | Sodium: 700mg | Vitamin A: 0µg | Vitamin B1: 0.1mg | Vitamin B2: 0.4mg | Vitamin B3: 8mg | Vitamin B5: 1mg | Vitamin B6: 0.5mg | Vitamin B7: 0µg | Vitamin B9: 10µg | Vitamin B12: 3µg | Iron: 2mg | Zinc: 3mg

Turkey tubes with bacon

Prep: 15 minutes | Cook: 30 minutes | Serves: 1

Ingredients:

- 1 turkey cutlet (7 oz) (200g)
- 2 slices bacon (50g)
- 1/2 cup heavy cream (120ml)
- 1/4 cup shredded cheese (30g)
- Salt to taste

Instructions:

1. Preheat the oven to 375°F (190°C).
2. Roll the turkey cutlet and wrap with bacon slices.
3. Place in a baking dish and pour heavy cream over the top.
4. Sprinkle it with shredded cheese.
5. Bake for 30 minutes, or until the turkey is cooked through and the cheese is golden.
6. Season with salt to taste before serving.

Nutritional Facts (Per Serving): Calories: 625 | Sugars: 0g | Fat: 45g | Carbs: 0g | Protein: 50g | Fiber: 0g | Sodium: 800mg | Vitamin A: 0µg | Vitamin B1: 0.1mg | Vitamin B2: 0.3mg | Vitamin B3: 8mg | Vitamin B5: 1.5mg | Vitamin B6: 0.9mg | Vitamin B7: 0µg | Vitamin B9: 12µg | Vitamin B12: 3µg | Iron: 2mg | Zinc: 3mg

Cheese soufflé with bacon

Prep: 15 minutes | Cook: 25 minutes | Serves: 1

Ingredients:

- 1/2 cup shredded cheese (60g)
- 2 large eggs, separated (100g)
- 2 slices bacon, cooked and crumbled (50g)
- 2 tbsp butter (30g)
- Salt to taste

Instructions:

1. Preheat the oven to 375°F (190°C).
2. Melt butter in a saucepan over medium heat, then mix in shredded cheese until smooth.
3. Remove from heat and stir in egg yolks, one at a time.
4. Beat egg whites until stiff peaks form, then gently fold into the cheese mixture. Fold in crumbled bacon.
5. Pour into a greased ramekin and bake for 25 minutes, or until puffed and golden.
6. Season with salt to taste before serving.

Nutritional Facts (Per Serving): Calories: 625 | Sugars: 0g | Fat: 50g | Carbs: 0g | Protein: 40g | Fiber: 0g | Sodium: 700mg | Vitamin A: 0µg | Vitamin B1: 0.1mg | Vitamin B2: 0.4mg | Vitamin B3: 7mg | Vitamin B5: 1mg | Vitamin B6: 0.5mg | Vitamin B7: 0µg | Vitamin B9: 10µg | Vitamin B12: 3µg | Iron: 1mg | Zinc: 2mg

CHAPTER 7: LUNCHES: Savory soups and best stew recipes

Seafood chowder

Prep: 15 minutes | Cook: 30 minutes | Serves: 1

Ingredients:

- 1/2 lb mixed seafood (225g)
- 1 cup heavy cream (240ml)
- 1/2 cup homemade fish or bone broth (120 мл)
- 1 tbsp butter (15g)
- Salt to taste

Instructions:

1. Melt butter in a large pot over medium heat.
2. Add seafood and cook until slightly opaque, 5-7 minutes.
3. Pour in the homemade broth and bring to a simmer.
4. Stir in heavy cream and cook until thickened, 15-20 minutes.
5. Season with salt and serve.

Nutritional Facts (Per Serving): Calories: 875 | Sugars: 0g | Fat: 65g | Carbs: 0g | Protein: 55g | Fiber: 0g | Sodium: 2000mg | Vitamin A: 450µg | Vitamin B1: 0.15mg | Vitamin B2: 0.3mg | Vitamin B3: 7.5mg | Vitamin B5: 1.25mg | Vitamin B6: 0.4mg | Vitamin B7: 0µg | Vitamin B9: 30µg | Vitamin B12: 5µg | Iron: 2.5mg | Zinc: 4mg

Creamy chicken liver soup

Prep: 10 minutes | Cook: 20 minutes | Serves: 1

Ingredients:

- 1/2 lb chicken livers (225g)
- 1 cup heavy cream (240ml)
- 1/2 cup homemade bone or meat broth (120 мл)
- 1 tbsp butter (15g)
- Salt to taste

Instructions:

1. Melt butter in a pot over medium heat.
2. Add chicken livers and cook until browned, 5-7 minutes.
3. Pour in homemade broth and bring to a boil.
4. Reduce heat and stir in heavy cream. Simmer until smooth and creamy, 10-15 minutes.
5. Season with salt and serve.

Nutritional Facts (Per Serving): Calories: 875 | Sugars: 0g | Fat: 65g | Carbs: 0g | Protein: 55g | Fiber: 0g | Sodium: 1800mg | Vitamin A: 7500µg | Vitamin B1: 1mg | Vitamin B2: 2mg | Vitamin B3: 13mg | Vitamin B5: 8mg | Vitamin B6: 1mg | Vitamin B7: 0µg | Vitamin B9: 600µg | Vitamin B12: 150µg | Iron: 13mg | Zinc: 8mg

Cream soup of beef and cheese

Prep: 10 minutes | Cook: 20 minutes | Serves: 1

Ingredients:

- 1/2 lb ground beef (225g)
- 1 cup heavy cream (240ml)
- 1/2 cup beef broth (120ml)
- 1/2 cup shredded cheddar cheese (50g)
- Salt to taste

Instructions:

1. Cook ground beef in a pot over medium heat until browned, 8-10 minutes.
2. Add beef broth and bring to a simmer.
3. Stir in heavy cream and shredded cheddar cheese until melted and smooth, 5-7 minutes.
4. Season with salt and serve.

Nutritional Facts (Per Serving): Calories: 875 | Sugars: 0g | Fat: 65g | Carbs: 0g | Protein: 55g | Fiber: 0g | Sodium: 1900mg | Vitamin A: 450µg | Vitamin B1: 0.1mg | Vitamin B2: 0.4mg | Vitamin B3: 4mg | Vitamin B5: 1.5mg | Vitamin B6: 0.4mg | Vitamin B7: 0µg | Vitamin B9: 20µg | Vitamin B12: 2.5µg | Iron: 5mg | Zinc: 10mg

Pork belly stew

Prep: 15 minutes | Cook: 1 hour | Serves: 1

Ingredients:

- 1/2 lb pork belly, diced (225g)
- 1 cup heavy cream (240ml)
- 1/2 cup chicken broth (120ml)
- 1 tbsp butter (15g)
- Salt to taste

Instructions:

1. Melt butter in a pot over medium heat.
2. Add diced pork belly and cook until browned, 10-12 minutes.
3. Pour in chicken broth and bring to a boil.
4. Reduce heat and stir in heavy cream. Simmer until pork belly is tender, 40-45 minutes.
5. Season with salt and serve.

Nutritional Facts (Per Serving): Calories: 875 | Sugars: 0g | Fat: 65g | Carbs: 0g | Protein: 55g | Fiber: 0g | Sodium: 2000mg | Vitamin A: 450µg | Vitamin B1: 0.2mg | Vitamin B2: 0.3mg | Vitamin B3: 5mg | Vitamin B5: 1.3mg | Vitamin B6: 0.4mg | Vitamin B7: 0µg | Vitamin B9: 15µg | Vitamin B12: 1.5µg | Iron: 2mg | Zinc: 4mg

Fish stew in clay pot

Prep: 15 minutes | Cook: 30 minutes | Serves: 1

Ingredients:

- 1/2 lb white fish fillets (225g)
- 1 cup heavy cream (240ml)
- 1/2 cup fish broth (120ml)
- 1 tbsp butter (15g)
- Salt to taste
- Fresh herbs (parsley, dill) to taste

Instructions:

1. Preheat oven to 375°F (190°C).
2. Melt butter in a clay pot over medium heat.
3. Add fish fillets and cook until slightly opaque, 5-7 minutes.
4. Pour in fish broth and bring to a simmer.
5. Stir in heavy cream and fresh herbs. Transfer to oven and bake for 20 minutes.
6. Season with salt and serve.

Nutritional Facts (Per Serving): Calories: 875 | Sugars: 0g | Fat: 65g | Carbs: 0g | Protein: 55g | Fiber: 0g | Sodium: 1900mg | Vitamin A: 300µg | Vitamin B1: 0.1mg | Vitamin B2: 0.3mg | Vitamin B3: 5mg | Vitamin B5: 0.3mg | Vitamin B6: 0.3mg | Vitamin B7: 0µg | Vitamin B9: 20µg | Vitamin B12: 3µg | Iron: 2mg | Zinc: 2mg

French cheese soup

Prep: 10 minutes | Cook: 20 minutes | Serves: 1

Ingredients:

- 2 oz bacon, diced (60g)
- 1 cup heavy cream (240ml)
- 1/2 cup chicken broth (120ml)
- 1/2 cup shredded Gruyère cheese (50g)
- Salt to taste

Instructions:

1. Cook bacon in a pot over medium heat until crispy, 5-7 minutes.
2. Add chicken broth and bring to a simmer.
3. Stir in heavy cream and shredded Gruyère cheese until melted and smooth, 10-12 minutes.
4. Season with salt and serve.

Nutritional Facts (Per Serving): Calories: 875 | Sugars: 0g | Fat: 65g | Carbs: 0g | Protein: 55g | Fiber: 0g | Sodium: 2000mg | Vitamin A: 450µg | Vitamin B1: 0.1mg | Vitamin B2: 0.3mg | Vitamin B3: 5mg | Vitamin B5: 1mg | Vitamin B6: 0.3mg | Vitamin B7: 0µg | Vitamin B9: 10µg | Vitamin B12: 1.5µg | Iron: 1mg | Zinc: 2mg

Lamb ragu italian-style

Prep: 15 minutes | Cook: 1 hours | Serves: 1

Ingredients:

- 1/2 lb lamb shoulder, diced (225g)
- 1 cup heavy cream (240ml)
- 1/2 cup beef broth (120ml)
- 1 tbsp butter (15g)
- Salt and Italian spices to taste

Instructions:

1. Melt butter in a pot over medium heat.
2. Add diced lamb shoulder and cook until browned, 10-12 minutes.
3. Pour in beef broth and bring to a boil.
4. Reduce heat and stir in heavy cream and Italian spices. Simmer until lamb is tender, 1.5 hours.
5. Season with salt and serve.

Nutritional Facts (Per Serving): Calories: 875 | Sugars: 0g | Fat: 65g | Carbs: 0g | Protein: 55g | Fiber: 0g | Sodium: 2000mg | Vitamin A: 450µg | Vitamin B1: 0.2mg | Vitamin B2: 0.3mg | Vitamin B3: 6mg | Vitamin B5: 1.5mg | Vitamin B6: 0.4mg | Vitamin B7: 0µg | Vitamin B9: 15µg | Vitamin B12: 2.5µg | Iron: 3mg | Zinc: 4mg

Braised beef tongue

Prep: 10 minutes | Cook: 1,5 hours | Serves: 1

Ingredients:

- 1/2 lb beef tongue, sliced (225g)
- 1 cup heavy cream (240ml)
- 1/2 cup beef broth (120ml)
- 1/2 cup shredded chedd cheese (50g)
- Salt to taste

Instructions:

1. Boil beef tongue in a pot for 1 hour, then pee and slice.
2. Melt butter in a pot over medium heat.
3. Add sliced beef tongue and cook until slightl browned, 10 minutes.
4. Pour in beef broth and bring to a simmer.
5. Stir in heavy cream and shredded chedda cheese until melted and smooth, 20-30 minutes.
6. Season with salt and serve.

Nutritional Facts (Per Serving): Calories: 875 | Sugars 0g | Fat: 65g | Carbs: 0g | Protein: 55g | Fiber: 0g Sodium: 2000mg | Vitamin A: 450µg | Vitamin B1: 0.1m | Vitamin B2: 0.3mg | Vitamin B3: 4mg | Vitamin B5 1.2mg | Vitamin B6: 0.3mg | Vitamin B7: 0µg | Vitami B9: 15µg | Vitamin B12: 2.5µg | Iron: 4mg | Zinc: 6mg

CHAPTER 8: LUNCHES: Meat lover's paradise: pork dishes for everyone

Stuffed pork zrazy

Prep: 15 minutes | Cook: 30 minutes | Serves: 1

Ingredients:

- 1 pork cutlet (7 oz) (200g)
- 2 oz cheese (60g), hard cheese without additives
- 22 oz roasted beef or chicken (60g),)
- Salt to taste

Instructions:

1. Preheat oven to 375°F (190°C).
2. Pound the pork cutlet thin and season with salt and pepper.
3. Place cheese and roasted meat (beef or chicken) on the pork cutlet, then roll it up and secure with toothpicks.
4. Grease a baking dish with ghee or beef tallow and place the roll in the dish. Bake for 25-30 minutes, until the pork is cooked through and the cheese is melted.

Nutritional Facts (Per Serving): Calories: 875 | Sugars: 0g | Fat: 60g | Carbs: 0g | Protein: 75g | Fiber: 0g | Sodium: 2000mg | Vitamin A: 0µg | Vitamin B1: 0.3mg | Vitamin B2: 0.4mg | Vitamin B3: 20mg | Vitamin B5: 2mg | Vitamin B6: 1mg | Vitamin B7: 0µg | Vitamin B9: 20µg | Vitamin B12: 3.5µg | Iron: 6mg | Zinc: 8mg

Cream pork chops

Prep: 10 minutes | Cook: 35 minutes | Serves: 1

Ingredients:

- 1 pork chop (7 oz) (200g)
- 2 oz shrimp, peeled (60g)
- 2 oz hard cheese (60g), without additives
- 1/4 cup heavy cream (60ml)
- Salt to taste

Instructions:

1. Preheat oven to 375°F (190°C).
2. Season the pork chop with salt and place in a baking dish.
3. Top with shrimp and cheese, then pour cream over the top.
4. Bake in the oven for 30-35 minutes until the pork is cooked through and the cheese is melted and bubbly.

Nutritional Facts (Per Serving): Calories: 875 | Sugars: 0g | Fat: 65g | Carbs: 0g | Protein: 65g | Fiber: 0g | Sodium: 2000mg | Vitamin A: 0µg | Vitamin B1: 0.3mg | Vitamin B2: 0.4mg | Vitamin B3: 20mg | Vitamin B5: 2mg | Vitamin B6: 1mg | Vitamin B7: 0µg | Vitamin B9: 20µg | Vitamin B12: 3.5µg | Iron: 6mg | Zinc: 8mg

Pork minced pockets

Prep: 15 minutes | Cook: 20 minutes | Serves: 1

Ingredients:

- 8 oz minced pork (240g)
- 4 slices of bacon (120g)
- Salt to taste

Instructions:

1. Preheat oven to 375°F (190°C).
2. Season the minced pork with salt and pepper, and shape into small patties.
3. Wrap each patty with bacon and secure with toothpicks.
4. Bake in the oven for 20-25 minutes until the pork is cooked through and the bacon is crispy.

Nutritional Facts (Per Serving): Calories: 875 | Sugars: 0g | Fat: 70g | Carbs: 0g | Protein: 55g | Fiber: 0g | Sodium: 2000mg | Vitamin A: 0µg | Vitamin B1: 0.3mg | Vitamin B2: 0.4mg | Vitamin B3: 20mg | Vitamin B5: 2mg | Vitamin B6: 1mg | Vitamin B7: 0µg | Vitamin B9: 20µg | Vitamin B12: 3.5µg | Iron: 6mg | Zinc: 8mg

Pork stew

Prep: 15 minutes | Cook: 1 hour | Serves: 1

Ingredients:

- 8 oz pork fillet (240g)
- 1/4 cup meat stock (60ml)
- Salt and pepper to taste

Instructions:

1. Preheat oven to 350°F (175°C).
2. Season the pork fillet with salt and pepper and place in a roasting pan.
3. Add meat stock and roast in the oven for 1 hour, basting occasionally, until tender.

Nutritional Facts (Per Serving): Calories: 875 | Sugars: 0g | Fat: 55g | Carbs: 0g | Protein: 75g | Fiber: 0g | Sodium: 2000mg | Vitamin A: 0µg | Vitamin B1: 0.3mg | Vitamin B2: 0.4mg | Vitamin B3: 20mg | Vitamin B5: 2mg | Vitamin B6: 1mg | Vitamin B7: 0µg | Vitamin B9: 20µg | Vitamin B12: 3.5µg | Iron: 6mg | Zinc: 8mg

Pork roll with chicken and cheese

Prep: 20 minutes | Cook: 20 minutes | Serves: 1

Ingredients:

- 8 oz minced pork (240g)
- 4 slices of bacon (120g)
- 2 oz cheese (60g), hard cheese without additive
- Salt and pepper to taste

Instructions:

1. Preheat oven to 375°F (190°C). Pound the pork fillet thin and season with salt and pepper.
2. Place chicken and cheese on the pork, roll up, and secure with toothpicks.
3. Bake in the oven for 30-35 minutes until the pork is cooked through and the cheese is melted.

Nutritional Facts (Per Serving): Calories: 875 | Sugars: 0g | Fat: 60g | Carbs: 0g | Protein: 75g | Fiber: 0g | Sodium: 2000mg | Vitamin A: 0µg | Vitamin B1: 0.3mg | Vitamin B2: 0.4mg | Vitamin B3: 20mg | Vitamin B5: 2mg | Vitamin B6: 1mg | Vitamin B7: 0µg | Vitamin B9: 20µg | Vitamin B12: 3.5µg | Iron: 6mg | Zinc: 8mg

Pork and lamb kebab with sauce

Prep: 20 minutes | Cook: 20 minutes | Serves: 1

Ingredients:

- 4 oz minced pork and lamb (120g each)
- 4 slices of bacon (120g)
- 1/4 cup homemade beef or bone broth (60ml)1/4
- Salt and pepper to taste

Instructions:

1. Mix minced pork and lamb together and season with salt and pepper.
2. Shape the mixture into kebabs and wrap with bacon slices.
3. Cook in a skillet over medium heat until browned and cooked through, about 10 minutes per side.
4. Serve with broth instead of peppercorn sauce for a more suitable carnivore-friendly version..

Nutritional Facts (Per Serving): Calories: 875 | Sugars: 0g | Fat: 70g | Carbs: 0g | Protein: 55g | Fiber: 0g | Sodium: 2000mg | Vitamin A: 0µg | Vitamin B1: 0.3mg | Vitamin B2: 0.4mg | Vitamin B3: 20mg | Vitamin B5: 2mg | Vitamin B6: 1mg | Vitamin B7: 0µg | Vitamin B9: 20µg | Vitamin B12: 3.5µg | Iron: 6mg | Zinc: 8mg

CHAPTER 9: LUNCHES: Meat lover's paradise: beef for the picky eaters

Classic roast beef

Prep: 10 minutes | Cook: 1 hour | Serves: 1

Ingredients:

- 8 oz beef roast (225g)
- 1/2 cup homemade beef broth (120ml)
- Salt and pepper to taste

Instructions:

1. Preheat oven to 375°F (190°C).
2. Season beef roast with salt and pepper.
3. Roast in the oven until medium-rare, about 1 hour.
3. Slice the roast and serve with the warm beef broth poured over as a sauce.

Nutritional Facts (Per Serving): Calories: 875 | Sugars: 0g | Fat: 62g | Carbs: 0g | Protein: 68g | Fiber: 0g | Sodium: 1200mg | Vitamin A: 0µg | Vitamin B1: 0.2mg | Vitamin B2: 0.3mg | Vitamin B3: 15mg | Vitamin B5: 1.5mg | Vitamin B6: 0.9mg | Vitamin B7: 0µg | Vitamin B9: 15µg | Vitamin B12: 2.7µg | Iron: 4.5mg | Zinc: 6mg

Beef stroganoff

Prep: 10 minutes | Cook: 20 minutes | Serves: 1

Ingredients:

- 8 oz beef sirloin, sliced (225g)
- 1/2 cup heavy cream (120ml)
- 1 tbsp butter (15g)
- Salt to taste

Instructions:

1. Melt butter in a skillet over medium heat.
2. Sear beef slices until browned, about 5 minutes.
3. Add heavy cream and simmer until sauce thickens, about 10 minutes.
4. Season with salt and serve.

Nutritional Facts (Per Serving): Calories: 875 | Sugars: 0g | Fat: 45g | Carbs: 0g | Protein: 60g | Fiber: 0g | Sodium: 200mg | Vitamin A: 0µg | Vitamin B1: 0.2mg | Vitamin B2: 0.3mg | Vitamin B3: 15mg | Vitamin B5: 1.5mg | Vitamin B6: 0.9mg | Vitamin B7: 0µg | Vitamin B9: 15µg | Vitamin B12: 2.7µg | Iron: 4.5mg | Zinc: 6mg

Baked beef in yogurt

Prep: 10 minutes | Cook: 30 minutes | Serves: 1

Ingredients:

- 8 oz beef chunks (225g)
- 1/2 cup full-fat Greek yogurt (120ml, no additives)
- Salt to taste

Instructions:

1. Preheat the oven to 375°F (190°C).
2. Mix beef chunks with Greek yogurt and salt.
3. Bake in the oven until beef is tender, about 30 minutes.
4. Serve alongside the yogurt.

Nutritional Facts (Per Serving): Calories: 875 | Sugars: 0g | Fat: 45g | Carbs: 0g | Protein: 60g | Fiber: 0g | Sodium: 200mg | Vitamin A: 0µg | Vitamin B1: 0.2mg | Vitamin B2: 0.3mg | Vitamin B3: 15mg | Vitamin B5: 1.5mg | Vitamin B6: 0.9mg | Vitamin B7: 0µg | Vitamin B9: 15µg | Vitamin B12: 2.7µg | Iron: 4.5mg | Zinc: 6mg

Butter-stuffed beef cutlet

Prep: 10 minutes | Cook: 15 minutes | Serves: 1

Ingredients:

- 8 oz ground beef (225g)
- 2 tbsp butter (30g)
- Salt to taste

Instructions:

1. Form ground beef into patties and stuff with butter.
2. Sear cutlets in a skillet over medium heat until browned, about 7-8 minutes per side.
3. Season with salt and serve.

Nutritional Facts (Per Serving): Calories: 875 | Sugars: 0g | Fat: 45g | Carbs: 0g | Protein: 60g | Fiber: 0g | Sodium: 200mg | Vitamin A: 0µg | Vitamin B1: 0.2mg | Vitamin B2: 0.3mg | Vitamin B3: 15mg | Vitamin B5: 1.5mg | Vitamin B6: 0.9mg | Vitamin B7: 0µg | Vitamin B9: 15µg | Vitamin B12: 2.7µg | Iron: 4.5mg | Zinc: 6mg

Cheesy chopped beefsteak

Prep: 10 minutes | Cook: 15 minutes | Serves: 1

Ingredients:

- 8 oz ground beef (225g)
- 2 oz cheddar cheese, sliced (60g)
- Salt to taste

Instructions:

1. Form ground beef into patties.
2. Sear patties in a skillet over medium heat until browned, about 7-8 minutes per side.
3. Top with cheddar cheese and let it melt.
4. Season with salt and serve.

Nutritional Facts (Per Serving): Calories: 875 | Sugars: 0g | Fat: 45g | Carbs: 0g | Protein: 60g | Fiber: 0g | Sodium: 200mg | Vitamin A: 0µg | Vitamin B1: 0.2mg | Vitamin B2: 0.3mg | Vitamin B3: 15mg | Vitamin B5: 1.5mg | Vitamin B6: 0.9mg | Vitamin B7: 0µg | Vitamin B9: 15µg | Vitamin B12: 2.7µg | Iron: 4.5mg | Zinc: 6mg

Pepper-crusted beef medallions

Prep: 10 minutes | Cook: 10 minutes | Serves: 1

Ingredients:

- 8 oz beef tenderloin, cut into medallions (225g)
- 1 tbsp cracked black pepper (15g)
- 1 tbsp butter (15g)
- Salt to taste

Instructions:

1. Press cracked pepper onto beef medallions.
2. Melt butter in a skillet over medium heat.
3. Sear medallions until desired doneness, about 4-5 minutes per side.
4. Season with salt and serve.

Nutritional Facts (Per Serving): Calories: 875 | Sugars: 0g | Fat: 45g | Carbs: 0g | Protein: 60g | Fiber: 0g | Sodium: 200mg | Vitamin A: 0µg | Vitamin B1: 0.2mg | Vitamin B2: 0.3mg | Vitamin B3: 15mg | Vitamin B5: 1.5mg | Vitamin B6: 0.9mg | Vitamin B7: 0µg | Vitamin B9: 15µg | Vitamin B12: 2.7µg | Iron: 4.5mg | Zinc: 6mg

CHAPTER 10: LUNCHES: Meat lover's paradise: quick and easy poultry dishes

Crispy chicken tabaka

Prep: 10 minutes | Cook: 25 minutes | Serves: 1

Ingredients:

- 1 whole chicken, flattened (2.2 lbs / 1kg)
- 2 tbsp butter (30g)
- Salt to taste

Instructions:

1. Season the flattened chicken with salt and pepper.
2. Heat butter in a large skillet over medium heat.
3. Place the chicken in the skillet, skin side down, and press with a weight.
4. Cook until golden and crispy, about 15 minutes per side.
5. Serve immediately.

Nutritional Facts (Per Serving): Calories: 875 | Sugars: g | Fat: 62g | Carbs: 0g | Protein: 71g | Fiber: 0g | Sodium: 2100mg | Vitamin A: 450µg | Vitamin B1: 0.1mg Vitamin B2: 0.2mg | Vitamin B3: 24mg | Vitamin B5: 6mg | Vitamin B6: 1.3mg | Vitamin B7: 0µg | Vitamin 9: 30µg | Vitamin B12: 1.6mg | Iron: 3.5mg | Zinc: 4mg

Chicken thighs with creamy sauce

Prep: 10 minutes | Cook: 30 minutes | Serves: 1

Ingredients:

- 4 chicken thighs (1 lb/450g)
- 1 cup heavy cream (240ml)
- 2 tbsp butter (30g)
- Salt and pepper to taste

Instructions:

1. Season chicken thighs with salt and pepper.
2. Melt butter in a skillet over medium heat.
3. Cook chicken thighs until browned and cooked through, about 7-8 minutes per side.
4. Remove thighs and add cream to the skillet, stirring to combine.
5. Simmer until the sauce thickens, about 5 minutes. Serve over chicken thighs.

Nutritional Facts (Per Serving): Calories: 875 | Sugars: 0g | Fat: 66g | Carbs: 0g | Protein: 62g | Fiber: 0g | Sodium: 1500mg | Vitamin A: 700µg | Vitamin B1: 0.1mg | Vitamin B2: 0.2mg | Vitamin B3: 22mg | Vitamin B5: 2.4mg | Vitamin B6: 1.2mg | Vitamin B7: 0µg | Vitamin B9: 28µg | Vitamin B12: 1.5µg | Iron: 3mg | Zinc: 3.5mg

Chicken fricassee

Prep: 10 minutes | Cook: 30 minutes | Serves: 1

Ingredients:

- 1 lb chicken pieces (450g)
- 1 cup heavy cream (240ml)
- 2 tbsp butter (30g)
- Salt and pepper to taste

Instructions:

1. Season chicken pieces with salt and pepper.
2. Melt butter in a skillet over medium heat.
3. Cook chicken until browned, about 5-6 minutes.
4. Add cream and simmer until the chicken is cooked through and the sauce thickens, about 20 minutes.
5. Serve hot.

Nutritional Facts (Per Serving): Calories: 875 | Sugars: 0g | Fat: 67g | Carbs: 0g | Protein: 59g | Fiber: 0g | Sodium: 1400mg | Vitamin A: 650µg | Vitamin B1: 0.1mg | Vitamin B2: 0.2mg | Vitamin B3: 21mg | Vitamin B5: 2.3mg | Vitamin B6: 1.1mg | Vitamin B7: 0µg | Vitamin B9: 25µg | Vitamin B12: 1.4µg | Iron: 3.2mg | Zinc: 3.6mg

Fillings from tongue and quail eggs

Prep: 15 minutes | Cook: 45 minutes | Serves: 1

Ingredients:

- 8 oz beef tongue, cooked and diced (225g)
- 6 quail eggs (90g)
- 2 tbsp butter (30g)
- Salt and pepper to taste

Instructions:

1. Melt butter in a skillet over medium heat.
2. Add beef tongue and cook until lightly browned about 5 minutes.
3. Add quail eggs and cook until whites are set about 3 minutes.
4. Season with salt and serve with clear beef broth

Nutritional Facts (Per Serving): Calories: 875 | Sugars 0g | Fat: 68g | Carbs: 0g | Protein: 60g | Fiber: 0g Sodium: 1600mg | Vitamin A: 300µg | Vitamin B1: 0.2m | Vitamin B2: 0.3mg | Vitamin B3: 15mg | Vitamin B5 2mg | Vitamin B6: 0.8mg | Vitamin B7: 0µg | Vitamin B9 20µg | Vitamin B12: 2.5µg | Iron: 5mg | Zinc: 5mg

Speedy chicken fingers

Prep 15 minutes | Cook: 10 minutes | Serves: 1

Ingredients:

- 8 oz chicken breast, cut into strips (225g)
- 1 cup grated cheese (120g), hard cheese with no additives
- 2 eggs, beaten (100g)
- 2 tbsp butter or bacon grease (30g)
- Salt and pepper to taste

Instructions:

1. Dip chicken strips in beaten eggs, then coat with grated cheese.

2. Heat butter or bacon grease in a skillet over medium heat.

3. Fry chicken strips until golden and cooked through, about 3-4 minutes per side.

4. Serve with peppercorn sauce or another sauce to taste.

Nutritional Facts (Per Serving): Calories: 875 | Sugars: 0g | Fat: 63g | Carbs: 0g | Protein: 70g | Fiber: 0g | Sodium: 2000mg | Vitamin A: 450µg | Vitamin B1: 0.2mg | Vitamin B2: 0.3mg | Vitamin B3: 20mg | Vitamin B5: 2.5mg | Vitamin B6: 1.2mg | Vitamin B7: 0µg | Vitamin B9: 22µg | Vitamin B12: 2.8µg | Iron: 3.6mg | Zinc: 4.2mg

Stuffed turkey patties

Prep: 15 minutes | Cook: 20 minutes | Serves: 1

Ingredients:

- 8 oz ground turkey (225g)
- 2 oz cheese, diced (60g), hard cheese without additives
- 2 tbsp butter (30g)
- Salt to taste

Instructions:

1. Form ground turkey into patties, placing diced cheese in the center.

2. Melt butter in a skillet over medium heat.

3. Cook patties until browned and cooked through, about 8-10 minutes per side.

4. Serve hot.

Nutritional Facts (Per Serving): Calories: 875 | Sugars: 0g | Fat: 61g | Carbs: 0g | Protein: 73g | Fiber: 0g | Sodium: 1700mg | Vitamin A: 400µg | Vitamin B1: 0.2mg | Vitamin B2: 0.3mg | Vitamin B3: 22mg | Vitamin B5: 2.4mg | Vitamin B6: 1.1mg | Vitamin B7: 0µg | Vitamin B9: 25µg | Vitamin B12: 2.7µg | Iron: 4mg | Zinc: 4.5mg

Chicken pudding

Prep: 10 minutes | Cook: 40 minutes | Serves: 1

Ingredients:

- 8 oz chicken breast, minced (225g)
- 1 cup heavy cream (240ml)
- 2 eggs (100g)
- Salt to taste

Instructions:

1. Preheat the oven to 350°F (175°C).
2. Mix minced chicken, heavy cream, and eggs. Season with salt.
3. Pour mixture into a greased baking dish.
Bake until set and golden, about 35-40 minutes.
4. Serve hot.

Nutritional Facts (Per Serving): Calories: 875 | Sugars: 0g | Fat: 68g | Carbs: 0g | Protein: 59g | Fiber: 0g | Sodium: 1500mg | Vitamin A: 700µg | Vitamin B1: 0.2mg | Vitamin B2: 0.3mg | Vitamin B3: 21mg | Vitamin B5: 2.5mg | Vitamin B6: 1mg | Vitamin B7: 0µg | Vitamin B9: 30µg | Vitamin B12: 2.6µg | Iron: 3mg | Zinc: 3.5mg

Bacon and cheese stuffed quail

Prep: 15 minutes | Cook: 25 minutes | Serves: 1

Ingredients:

- 2 quail (200g)
- 2 slices bacon, diced (60g)
- 2 oz cheese, diced (60g)
- Salt to taste

Instructions:

1. Preheat oven to 375°F (190°C).
2. Remove the bones from the quail. Stuff the quail with the diced bacon and cheese
3. Season with salt and place in a baking dish.
Bake until golden and cooked through, about 20-25 minutes.
4. Serve hot.

Nutritional Facts (Per Serving): Calories: 875 | Sugars: 0g | Fat: 64g | Carbs: 0g | Protein: 65g | Fiber: 0g | Sodium: 1800mg | Vitamin A: 350µg | Vitamin B1: 0.2mg | Vitamin B2: 0.3mg | Vitamin B3: 19mg | Vitamin B5: 2.2mg | Vitamin B6: 0.9mg | Vitamin B7: 0µg | Vitamin B9: 25µg | Vitamin B12: 2.4µg | Iron: 4.2mg | Zinc: 4.7mg

Beef tartare with cheese

Prep: 10 minutes | Cook: 5 minutes | Serves: 1

Ingredients:

- 4 oz finely chopped raw beef (115g)
- 1 egg yolk (20g)
- 1 oz hard cheese, sliced (30g)
- Pepper to taste

Instructions:

1. Mix finely chopped beef with the egg yolk.
2. Arrange the beef mixture on a plate and top with hard cheese slices.
3. Season with black pepper.
4. Serve immediately.

Nutritional Facts (Per Serving): Calories: 375 | Sugars: minimal | Fat: 26g | Carbs: 0g | Protein: 18g | Fiber: 0g | Sodium: 500mg | Vitamin A: 110µg | Vitamin B1: 0.163mg | Vitamin B2: 0.165mg | Vitamin B3: 2.4mg NE | Vitamin B5: 0.75mg | Vitamin B6: 0.195mg | Vitamin B7: 5µg | Vitamin B9: 9µg | Vitamin B12: 1.62µg | Iron: 2.7mg | Zinc: 3.6mg

Salmon tartare with egg sauce

Prep: 10 minutes | Cook: 5 minutes | Serves: 1

Ingredients:

- 4 oz finely chopped raw salmon (115g)
- 1 egg yolk (20g)
- Salt and pepper to taste

Instructions:

1. Mix finely chopped salmon with the egg yolk.
2. Season with salt and pepper.
3. Serve immediately.

Nutritional Facts (Per Serving): Calories: 375 | Sugars: minimal | Fat: 25g | Carbs: 0g | Protein: 18g | Fiber: 0g | Sodium: 500mg | Vitamin A: 130µg | Vitamin B1: 0.164mg | Vitamin B2: 0.165mg | Vitamin B3: 2.3mg NE | Vitamin B5: 0.74mg | Vitamin B6: 0.194mg | Vitamin B7: 4.4µg | Vitamin B9: 8µg | Vitamin B12: 1.61µg | Iron: 2.6mg | Zinc: 3.5mg

Meat boats with eggs

Prep: 15 minutes | Cook: 15 minutes | Serves: 1

Ingredients:

- 8 oz minced meat (225g)
- 1 oz cheese, grated (30g)
- 1 egg (50g)
- Salt and pepper to taste

Instructions:

1. Form minced meat into boat shapes and place in a frying pan.
2. Crack an egg into each meat boat and sprinkle with grated cheese.
3. Fry over medium heat until the meat is cooked and the egg is set, about 10-15 minutes.
4. Season with salt and pepper. Serve immediately.

Nutritional Facts (Per Serving): Calories: 375 | Sugars: minimal | Fat: 27g | Carbs: 0g | Protein: 18g | Fiber: 0g | Sodium: 500mg | Vitamin A: 120µg | Vitamin B1: 0.165mg | Vitamin B2: 0.165mg | Vitamin B3: 2.4mg NE | Vitamin B5: 0.75mg | Vitamin B6: 0.195mg | Vitamin B7: 4.5µg | Vitamin B9: 9µg | Vitamin B12: 1.62µg | Iron: 2.7mg | Zinc: 3.6mg

Chicken julienne

Prep: 10 minutes | Cook: 20 minutes | Serves: 1

Ingredients:

- 8 oz chicken breast, sliced (225g)
- 1 cup heavy cream (240ml)
- 2 tbsp butter (30g)
- Salt and pepper to taste

Instructions:

1. Melt butter in a skillet over medium heat.
2. Add chicken slices and cook until lightl browned, about 5-7 minutes.
3. Add heavy cream and simmer until the sauc thickens, about 10-12 minutes.
4. Season with salt and pepper. Serve hot.

Nutritional Facts (Per Serving): Calories: 375 | Sugars minimal | Fat: 27g | Carbs: 0g | Protein: 18g | Fiber: 0g Sodium: 500mg | Vitamin A: 125µg | Vitamin B1 0.163mg | Vitamin B2: 0.165mg | Vitamin B3: 2.3mg NE Vitamin B5: 0.74mg | Vitamin B6: 0.194mg | Vitamin B7 4.4µg | Vitamin B9: 8µg | Vitamin B12: 1.61µg | Iron 2.6mg | Zinc: 3.5m

Bacon-wrapped shrimp skewers

Prep: 15 minutes | Cook: 15 minutes | Serves: 1

Ingredients:

- 6 large shrimp, peeled and deveined (90g)
- 3 slices of bacon (90g)
- Salt and pepper to taste

Instructions:

1. Wrap each shrimp with a slice of bacon and skewer.
2. Grill on a grill pan over medium heat until bacon is crispy and shrimp are cooked, about 3-4 minutes per side.
3. Season with salt and pepper.
4. Serve hot.

Nutritional Facts (Per Serving): Calories: 375 | Sugars: minimal | Fat: 27g | Carbs: 0g | Protein: 18g | Fiber: 0g | Sodium: 500mg | Vitamin A: 110µg | Vitamin B1: 0.164mg | Vitamin B2: 0.165mg | Vitamin B3: 2.2mg NE | Vitamin B5: 0.74mg | Vitamin B6: 0.194mg | Vitamin B7: 4.4µg | Vitamin B9: 8µg | Vitamin B12: 1.61µg | Iron: 2.5mg | Zinc: 3.5mg

Deep-fried pork

Prep: 10 minutes | Cook: 15 minutes | Serves: 1

Ingredients:

- 8 oz thin strips of pork (225g)
- 2 tbsp lard or butter (30g)
- Salt and pepper to taste

Instructions:

1. Heat lard or butter in a deep fryer or deep skillet over medium heat.
2. Fry pork strips until golden and crispy, about 5-7 minutes.
3. Drain on paper towels and season with salt and pepper.
4. Serve with meat sauce.

Nutritional Facts (Per Serving): Calories: 375 | Sugars: minimal | Fat: 27g | Carbs: 0g | Protein: 18g | Fiber: 0g | Sodium: 500mg | Vitamin A: 120µg | Vitamin B1: 0.165mg | Vitamin B2: 0.165mg | Vitamin B3: 2.4mg NE | Vitamin B5: 0.75mg | Vitamin B6: 0.195mg | Vitamin B7: 4.5µg | Vitamin B9: 9µg | Vitamin B12: 1.62µg | Iron: 2.7mg | Zinc: 3.6m

Cheese balls with slices of boiled ham

Prep: 10 minutes | Cook: 10 minutes | Serves: 1

Ingredients:

- 4 oz cheese, grated (115g)
- 2 oz boiled ham, diced (60g)
- 1 egg (50g)
- Salt to taste

Instructions:

1. Mix grated cheese, diced ham, and egg to form a dough.
2. Shape into small balls.
3. Fry in a skillet over medium heat until golden and crispy, about 5-7 minutes.
4. Season with salt and serve with a sauce of your choice.

Nutritional Facts (Per Serving): Calories: 375 | Sugars: minimal | Fat: 27g | Carbs: 0g | Protein: 18g | Fiber: 0g | Sodium: 500mg | Vitamin A: 110µg | Vitamin B1: 0.164mg | Vitamin B2: 0.165mg | Vitamin B3: 2.3mg NE | Vitamin B5: 0.74mg | Vitamin B6: 0.194mg | Vitamin B7: 4.4µg | Vitamin B9: 8µg | Vitamin B12: 1.61µg | Iron: 2.6mg | Zinc: 3.5mg

Egg and cheese tacos with meat filling

Prep: 10 minutes | Cook: 15 minutes | Serves: 1

Ingredients:

- 2 eggs, beaten (100g)
- 2 oz grated cheese (60g)
- 4 oz chicken breast, sliced (115g)
- 4 oz beef strips (115g)
- 2 tbsp butter (30g)
- Salt to taste

Instructions:

1. Cook chicken breast and beef strips in butter until done, about 7-8 minutes.
2. In a separate pan, cook beaten eggs to form two thin omelets.
3. Place meat filling on one half of each omelet, sprinkle with grated cheese, and fold over to form tacos.
4. Cook for an additional 2-3 minutes until cheese is melted.
5. Season with salt. Serve immediately.

Nutritional Facts (Per Serving): Calories: 375 | Sugars: minimal | Fat: 27g | Carbs: 0g | Protein: 18g | Fiber: 0g | Sodium: 500mg | Vitamin A: 125µg | Vitamin B1: 0.165mg | Vitamin B2: 0.165mg | Vitamin B3: 2.4mg NE | Vitamin B5: 0.75mg | Vitamin B6: 0.195mg | Vitamin B7: 4.5µg | Vitamin B9: 9µg | Vitamin B12: 1.62µg | Iron: 2.7mg | Zinc: 3.6mg

Steak and egg salad

Prep: 10 minutes | Cook: 10 minutes | Serves: 1

Ingredients:

- 4 oz beef steak, thinly sliced (115g)
- 2 slices bacon, fried and crumbled (60g)
- 1 oz hard cheese, grated (30g)
- 4 quail eggs, boiled (60g)
- 2 tbsp heavy cream (30ml)
- 1 large egg (50g)
- Salt and pepper to taste

Instructions:

1. Cook beef steak to desired doneness and slice thinly.
2. Mix beef, crumbled bacon, grated cheese, and quail eggs in a bowl.
3. In a small pan, heat the heavy cream and add the large egg, whisking until the dressing thickens.
4. Season with salt and pepper.
5. Drizzle the dressing over the salad and serve.

Nutritional Facts (Per Serving): Calories: 375 | Sugars: minimal | Fat: 27g | Carbs: 0g | Protein: 17g | Fiber: 0g | Sodium: 500mg | Vitamin A: 110μg | Vitamin B1: 0.165mg | Vitamin B2: 0.163mg | Vitamin B3: 2.4mg NE | Vitamin B5: 0.75mg | Vitamin B6: 0.195mg | Vitamin B7: .5mg | Vitamin B9: 9μg | Vitamin B12: 1.62μg | Iron: .7mg | Zinc: 3.6mg

Salad with chicken, shrimp, cheese, and egg

Prep: 10 minutes | Cook: 10 minutes | Serves: 1

Ingredients:

- 3 oz chicken breast, cooked and diced (85g)
- 2 oz boiled shrimp (60g)
- 1 oz cheddar cheese, grated (30g)
- 1 large egg, boiled and diced (50g)
- 2 tbsp butter, melted (30g)
- Salt and pepper to taste

Instructions:

1. Combine chicken, shrimp, cheddar cheese, and boiled egg in a bowl.
2. Drizzle with melted butter and season with salt and pepper. Toss to combine.
3. Serve immediately.

Nutritional Facts (Per Serving): Calories: 375 | Sugars: minimal | Fat: 26g | Carbs: 0g | Protein: 18g | Fiber: 0g | Sodium: 500mg | Vitamin A: 115μg | Vitamin B1: 0.164mg | Vitamin B2: 0.165mg | Vitamin B3: 2.3mg NE | Vitamin B5: 0.74mg | Vitamin B6: 0.194mg | Vitamin B7: 4.4mg | Vitamin B9: 8μg | Vitamin B12: 1.61μg | Iron: 2.6mg | Zinc: 3.5mg

Salad with fried pork ham, goat cheese, and poached egg

Prep: 10 minutes | Cook: 10 minutes | Serves: 1

Ingredients:

- 3 oz pork ham, fried and diced (85g)
- 1 oz goat cheese, crumbled (30g)
- 1 large egg, poached (50g)
- 2 tbsp bacon sauce (30ml)
- Salt and pepper to taste

Instructions:

1. Combine fried pork ham and goat cheese in a bowl.
2. Top with a poached egg.
3. Drizzle with bacon sauce and season with salt and pepper.
4. Serve immediately.

Nutritional Facts (Per Serving): Calories: 375 | Sugars: minimal | Fat: 25g | Carbs: 0g | Protein: 18g | Fiber: 0g | Sodium: 500mg | Vitamin A: 120µg | Vitamin B1: 0.164mg | Vitamin B2: 0.165mg | Vitamin B3: 2.2mg NE | Vitamin B5: 0.73mg | Vitamin B6: 0.193mg | Vitamin B7: 4.3mg | Vitamin B9: 7µg | Vitamin B12: 1.60µg | Iron: 2.5mg | Zinc: 3.4mg

Pork chop salad with hard cheese and bacon

Prep: 10 minutes | Cook: 10 minutes | Serves: 1

Ingredients:

- 4 oz pork chop, cooked and sliced (115g)
- 2 slices bacon, fried and crumbled (60g)
- 1 oz hard cheese, grated (30g)
- 2 tbsp bacon sauce (30ml)
- Salt and pepper to taste

Instructions:

1. Combine sliced pork chop, crumbled bacon, and grated cheese in a bowl.
2. Drizzle with bacon sauce and season with salt and pepper.
3. Serve immediately.

Nutritional Facts (Per Serving): Calories: 375 | Sugars: minimal | Fat: 27g | Carbs: 0g | Protein: 17g | Fiber: 0g | Sodium: 500mg | Vitamin A: 108µg | Vitamin B1: 0.163mg | Vitamin B2: 0.163mg | Vitamin B3: 2.1mg NE | Vitamin B5: 0.73mg | Vitamin B6: 0.193mg | Vitamin B7: 4.3mg | Vitamin B9: 7µg | Vitamin B12: 1.60µg | Iron: 2.5mg | Zinc: 3.4mg

Variation of the salad "Cobb" with duck breast for Carnivore Diet

Prep: 10 minutes | Cook: 20 minutes | Serves: 1

Ingredients:

- 4 oz roasted duck breast, sliced (115g)
- 2 large eggs, hard-boiled and diced (100g)
- 1 oz cream cheese (30g)
- 2 tbsp heavy cream (30ml)
- Salt and pepper to taste

Instructions:

1. Combine sliced duck breast and diced hard-boiled eggs in a bowl.

2. In a small pan, melt cream cheese with heavy cream, stirring until smooth.

3. Drizzle the cream cheese sauce over the salad and season with salt and pepper.

4. Serve immediately.

Nutritional Facts (Per Serving): Calories: 375 | Sugars: minimal | Fat: 25g | Carbs: 0g | Protein: 18g | Fiber: 0g | Sodium: 500mg | Vitamin A: 135µg | Vitamin B1: 0.165mg | Vitamin B2: 0.165mg | Vitamin B3: 2.4mg NE | Vitamin B5: 0.75mg | Vitamin B6: 0.195mg | Vitamin B7: 4.5mg | Vitamin B9: 9µg | Vitamin B12: 1.62µg | Iron: 2.7mg | Zinc: 3.6mg

Cheese salad

Prep: 10 minutes | Cook: 10 minutes | Serves: 1

Ingredients:

- 1 oz cheddar cheese, grated (30g)
- 1 oz curd cheese (30g)
- 2 tbsp sour cream (30ml)
- 3 oz chicken breast, fried and sliced (85g)
- Salt and pepper to taste

Instructions:

1. Add the cheddar cheese, curd and sour cream to a bowl. Sauté with salt and black pepper.

2. Slice the fried chicken.

2. Mix everything on a plate and serve with sour cream, cheese sauce or sauce Béarnaise.

Nutritional Facts (Per Serving): Calories: 375 | Sugars: minimal | Fat: 26g | Carbs: 0g | Protein: 16g | Fiber: 0g | Sodium: 500mg | Vitamin A: 120µg | Vitamin B1: 0.163mg | Vitamin B2: 0.163mg | Vitamin B3: 2.2mg NE | Vitamin B5: 0.73mg | Vitamin B6: 0.193mg | Vitamin B7: 4.3mg | Vitamin B9: 7µg | Vitamin B12: 1.60µg | Iron: 2.5mg | Zinc: 3.4mg

Beef bone broth

Prep: 10 minutes | Cook: 8 hours | Serves: 1

Ingredients:

- 1 lb beef bones (450g)
- 8 cups water (2 liters)
- 1 tsp sea salt (5g)

Instructions:

1. Place beef bones in a large pot and cover with water.
2. Add sea salt and bring to a boil.
3/ Reduce heat and simmer for 8 hours.
4. Strain the broth and serve.

Nutritional Facts (Per Serving): Calories: 375 | Sugars: 0g | Fat: 27g | Carbs: 0g | Protein: 16g | Fiber: 0g | Sodium: 500mg | Vitamin A: 120µg | Vitamin B1: 0.164mg | Vitamin B2: 0.164mg | Vitamin B3: 2.3mg NE | Vitamin B5: 0.74mg | Vitamin B6: 0.194mg | Vitamin B7: 4.4mg | Vitamin B9: 8µg | Vitamin B12: 1.61µg | Iron: 2.6mg | Zinc: 3.5mg

Chicken bone broth with egg and chicken breast

Prep: 10 minutes | Cook: 6 hours | Serves: 1

Ingredients:

- 1 lb chicken bones (450g)
- 1 hard boiled egg, chopped (50g)
- 4 oz chicken breast, cooked and shredded (115g)
- 8 cups water (2 liters)
- 1 tsp sea salt (5g)

Instructions:

1. Place chicken bones in a large pot and cover with water.
2. Add sea salt and bring to a boil.
3. Reduce heat and simmer for 6 hours.
4. Strain the broth, add chopped egg and shredded chicken breast. Serve hot.

Nutritional Facts (Per Serving): Calories: 375 | Sugars: 0g | Fat: 26g | Carbs: 0g | Protein: 17g | Fiber: 0g | Sodium: 500mg | Vitamin A: 110µg | Vitamin B1: 0.165mg | Vitamin B2: 0.165mg | Vitamin B3: 2.2mg NE | Vitamin B5: 0.73mg | Vitamin B6: 0.193mg | Vitamin B7: 4.3mg | Vitamin B9: 8µg | Vitamin B12: 1.60µg | Iron: 2.5mg | Zinc: 3.4mg

Pork bone broth with meatballs

Prep: 10 minutes | Cook: 8 hours | Serves: 1

Ingredients:

- 1 lb pork bones (450g)
- 4 oz ground pork, formed into meatballs (115g)
- 8 cups water (2 liters)
- 1 tsp sea salt (5g)

Instructions:

1. Place pork bones in a large pot and cover with water.
2. Add sea salt and bring to a boil.
3. Reduce heat and simmer for 8 hours.
4. Strain the broth, add pork meatballs, and cook until meatballs are done, about 10 minutes.
5. Serve hot.

Nutritional Facts (Per Serving): Calories: 375 | Sugars: ?g | Fat: 27g | Carbs: 0g | Protein: 16g | Fiber: 0g | Sodium: 500mg | Vitamin A: 115µg | Vitamin B1: 0.164mg | Vitamin B2: 0.164mg | Vitamin B3: 2.3mg NE | Vitamin B5: 0.75mg | Vitamin B6: 0.195mg | Vitamin B7: ?.4mg | Vitamin B9: 7µg | Vitamin B12: 1.62µg | Iron: ?.7mg | Zinc: 3.6mg

Carnivore shurpa without vegetables

Prep: 10 minutes | Cook: 3 hours | Serves: 1

Ingredients:

- 1 lb beef or lamb (450g)
- 2 quail or 1 wild duck, cleaned and halved (200g)
- 1 tsp sea salt (5g)
- 1 tsp peppercorns (5g)
- 1/2 cup heavy cream (optional, for serving) (120ml)

Instructions:

1. Place the beef or lamb, quail or wild duck, sea salt, peppercorns in a large pot.
2. Bring to a boil, then reduce heat and simmer for 3 hours.
3. Strain the broth and serve with heavy cream if desired.

Nutritional Facts (Per Serving): Calories: 375 | Sugars: minimal | Fat: 26g | Carbs: 0g | Protein: 17g | Fiber: 0g | Sodium: 500mg | Vitamin A: 135µg | Vitamin B1: 0.165mg | Vitamin B2: 0.165mg | Vitamin B3: 2.4mg NE | Vitamin B5: 0.75mg | Vitamin B6: 0.195mg | Vitamin B7: 4.5mg | Vitamin B9: 9µg | Vitamin B12: 1.62µg | Iron: 2.7mg | Zinc: 3.6mg

Chicken liver pâté

Prep: 15 minutes | Cook: 20 minutes | Serves: 1

Ingredients:

- 6 oz chicken liver (170g)
- 2 tbsp butter (30g)
- 2 boiled eggs (100g)
- 2 oz salted curd cheese (60g)

Instructions:

1. Melt butter in a skillet over medium heat. Add chicken liver and cook until browned and cooked through, about 7-10 minutes.
2. Blend the cooked liver with the butter until smooth.
3. Serve the pâté with boiled eggs and salted curd cheese mousse.

Nutritional Facts (Per Serving): Calories: 375 | Sugars: minimal | Fat: 27g | Carbs: 0g | Protein: 18g | Fiber: 0g | Sodium: 500mg | Vitamin A: 135µg | Vitamin B1: 0.165mg | Vitamin B2: 0.165mg | Vitamin B3: 2.4mg NE | Vitamin B5: 0.75mg | Vitamin B6: 0.195mg | Vitamin B7: 4.5mg | Vitamin B9: 9µg | Vitamin B12: 1.62µg | Iron: 2.7mg | Zinc: 3.6mg

Béchamel sauce

Prep: 5 minutes | Cook: 10 minutes | Serves: 1

Ingredients:

- 1 cup buttered milk (240ml)
- 1 tsp gelatin (5g)
- Salt to taste

Instructions:

1. Heat buttered milk in a saucepan over medium heat.
2. Add gelatin and stir until fully dissolved.
3. Season with salt and serve. Serve it to chicken other bird and dishes from it.

Nutritional Facts (Per Serving): Calories: 375 | Sugars minimal | Fat: 26g | Carbs: 0g | Protein: 17g | Fiber: 0g Sodium: 500mg | Vitamin A: 120µg | Vitamin B1 0.163mg | Vitamin B2: 0.163mg | Vitamin B3: 2.3mg NE Vitamin B5: 0.74mg | Vitamin B6: 0.193mg | Vitamin B7 4.4mg | Vitamin B9: 8µg | Vitamin B12: 1.61µg | Iron 2.6mg | Zinc: 3.5mg

Hollandaise sauce

Prep: 5 minutes | Cook: 5 minutes | Serves: 1

Ingredients:

- 2 egg yolks (40g)
- 1/2 cup butter (120g))
- Salt to taste

Instructions:

1. Whisk egg yolks a heatproof bowl.
2. Place the bowl over a pot of simmering water and slowly add melted butter while whisking continuously until thickened.
3. Season with salt and serve. Serve with fish and egg dishes.

Nutritional Facts (Per Serving): Calories: 375 | Sugars: minimal | Fat: 27g | Carbs: 0g | Protein: 17g | Fiber: 0g | Sodium: 500mg | Vitamin A: 135µg | Vitamin B1: 0.165mg | Vitamin B2: 0.165mg | Vitamin B3: 2.4mg NE | Vitamin B5: 0.75mg | Vitamin B6: 0.195mg | Vitamin B7: 4.5mg | Vitamin B9: 9µg | Vitamin B12: 1.62µg | Iron: 2.7mg | Zinc: 3.6mg

Peppercorn sauce

Prep: 5 minutes | Cook: 15 minutes | Serves: 1

Ingredients:

- 1/2 cup heavy cream (120ml)
- 1/2 cup beef broth (120ml))
- 1 tbsp black peppercorns, crushed (15g)

Instructions:

1. Combine cream, beef broth, and crushed peppercorns in a saucepan over medium heat.
2. Simmer until the sauce thickens, about 10-15 minutes.
3. Serve hot, ideally over steaks or other cuts of meat..

Nutritional Facts (Per Serving): Calories: 375 | Sugars: minimal | Fat: 25g | Carbs: 0g | Protein: 16g | Fiber: 0g | Sodium: 500mg | Vitamin A: 108µg | Vitamin B1: 0.163mg | Vitamin B2: 0.163mg | Vitamin B3: 2.1mg NE | Vitamin B5: 0.73mg | Vitamin B6: 0.193mg | Vitamin B7: 4.3mg | Vitamin B9: 7µg | Vitamin B12: 1.60µg | Iron: 2.5mg | Zinc: 3.4mg

Béarnaise sauce

Prep: 5 minutes | Cook: 10 minutes | Serves: 1

Ingredients:

- 2 egg yolks (40g)
- 1/2 cup butter (120g)
- 2 tbsp beef bone broth (30ml)
- Salt to taste

Instructions:

1. Whisk the egg yolks and warm beef bone broth in a heatproof bowl.
2. Place the bowl over a pot of simmering water, whisking continuously as you slowly add melted butter until thickened. Season with salt to taste.
3. Serve with steak, seafood, chicken, or grilled dishes.

Nutritional Facts (Per Serving): Calories: 375 | Sugars: minimal | Fat: 27g | Carbs: 0g | Protein: 16g | Fiber: 0g | Sodium: 500mg | Vitamin A: 135µg | Vitamin B1: 0.165mg | Vitamin B2: 0.165mg | Vitamin B3: 2.4mg NE | Vitamin B5: 0.75mg | Vitamin B6: 0.195mg | Vitamin B7: 4.5mg | Vitamin B9: 9µg | Vitamin B12: 1.62µg | Iron: 2.7mg | Zinc: 3.6mg

Pork Lard Chimichurri

Prep: 5 minutes | Cook: 0 minutes | Serves: 1

Ingredients:

- 3 tbsp pork lard, melted (45ml))
- 1/2 tsp salt (2.5g)
- 1/2 tsp black pepper (1g)
- 1/2 tsp red pepper flakes (1g)

Instructions:

1 In a small mixing bowl, blend the melted pork lard.
2 Season the mixture with salt, black pepper, and red pepper flakes.
3 Whisk thoroughly until the ingredients are fully combined.
4 Let the chimichurri rest for at least 10 minutes for the flavors to blend.
5 Serve as a topping for grilled meats or use as a marinade

Nutritional Facts (Per Serving): Calories: 375 | Sugars: 0g | Fat: 40g | Carbohydrates: 1g | Protein: 1g | Fiber: 0g | Sodium: 500mg | Vitamin A: 0µg | Vitamin B1: 0mg | Vitamin B2: 0mg | Vitamin B3: 0mg | Vitamin B5: 0mg | Vitamin B6: 0mg | Vitamin B7: 0µg | Vitamin B9: 0µg | Vitamin B12: 0µg | Iron: 0mg | Zinc: 0mg

CHAPTER 15: INSTEAD OF DESSERTS: dairy products for meat-eaters

Emmental and mascarpone cheesecake

Prep: 15 minutes | Cook: 30 minutes | Serves: 1

Ingredients:

- 2 oz mascarpone (60g)
- 2 oz grated Emmental cheese (60g)
- 2 oz cottage cheese (60g)

Instructions:

1. Preheat oven to 350°F (175°C).
2. Mix mascarpone, Emmental, and cottage cheese until smooth.
3. Pour the mixture into a greased baking dish.
4. Bake until set and golden, about 30 minutes.
5. Let cool before serving.

Nutritional Facts (Per Serving): Calories: 375 | Sugars: minimal | Fat: 27g | Carbs: 0g | Protein: 17g | Fiber: 0g | Sodium: 500mg | Vitamin A: 120μg | Vitamin B1: 0.165mg | Vitamin B2: 0.165mg | Vitamin B3: 2.4mg NE | Vitamin B5: 0.75mg | Vitamin B6: 0.195mg | Vitamin B7: 4.5mg | Vitamin B9: 9μg | Vitamin B12: 1.62μg | Iron: 2.7mg | Zinc: 3.6mg

Milk and ricotta pudding

Prep: 15 minutes | Cook: chill for 2 hours | Serves: 1

Ingredients:

- 4 oz ricotta cheese (120g)
- 2 oz mascarpone (60g)
- 4 oz whole milk (120ml)

Instructions:

1. Blend ricotta, mascarpone, and milk until smooth.
Pour mixture into a serving dish.
2. Chill in the refrigerator for at least 2 hours before serving.

Nutritional Facts (Per Serving): Calories: 375 | Sugars: minimal | Fat: 26g | Carbs: 0g | Protein: 17g | Fiber: 0g | Sodium: 500mg | Vitamin A: 130μg | Vitamin B1: 0.163mg | Vitamin B2: 0.163mg | Vitamin B3: 2.2mg NE | Vitamin B5: 0.73mg | Vitamin B6: 0.193mg | Vitamin B7: 4.3mg | Vitamin B9: 7μg | Vitamin B12: 1.60μg | Iron: 2.5mg | Zinc: 3.4mg

Milkshake with cheddar

Prep: 5 minutes | Cook:10 minutes | Serves: 1

Ingredients:

- 1 cup whole milk (240ml)
- 2 oz heavy cream (60ml)
- 1 oz grated cheddar (30g)

Instructions:

1. Blend milk, heavy cream, and grated cheddar until smooth.
2. Pour into a glass and serve immediately.

Nutritional Facts (Per Serving): Calories: 375 | Sugars: minimal | Fat: 27g | Carbs: 0g | Protein: 16g | Fiber: 0g | Sodium: 500mg | Vitamin A: 135µg | Vitamin B1: 0.165mg | Vitamin B2: 0.165mg | Vitamin B3: 2.4mg NE | Vitamin B5: 0.75mg | Vitamin B6: 0.195mg | Vitamin B7: 4.5mg | Vitamin B9: 9µg | Vitamin B12: 1.62µg | Iron: 2.7mg | Zinc: 3.6mg

Cottage cheese casserole with cream

Prep: 10 minutes | Cook: 25 minutes | Serves: 1

Ingredients:

- 4 oz cottage cheese (120g)
- 2 oz heavy cream (60ml)

Instructions:

1. Preheat oven to 350°F (175°C).
2. Mix cottage cheese and heavy cream until combined.
3. Pour mixture into a greased baking dish.
4. Bake until set and golden, about 25 minutes.
5. Let cool slightly before serving.

Nutritional Facts (Per Serving): : Calories: 375 Sugars: minimal | Fat: 26g | Carbs: 0g | Protein: 16g Fiber: 0g | Sodium: 500mg | Vitamin A: 125µg | Vitamin B1: 0.164mg | Vitamin B2: 0.164mg | Vitamin B3: 2.3mg NE | Vitamin B5: 0.74mg | Vitamin B6: 0.194mg | Vitamin B7: 4.4mg | Vitamin B9: 8µg | Vitamin B12: 1.61µg | Iron 2.6mg | Zinc: 3.5m

CHAPTER 16: DINNER: Dishes in one pan

Pan-fried shrimp with cheese sauce

Prep: 10 minutes | Cook: 15 minutes | Serves: 1

Ingredients:

- 8 oz shrimp (225g)
- 2 tbsp butter (30g)
- 1/4 cup heavy cream (60ml)
- 1/4 cup grated cheese (60g)
- Salt and pepper to taste

Instructions:

1. Melt butter in a skillet over medium heat.
2. Add shrimp and cook until pink and opaque, about 3-4 minutes per side.
3. Remove shrimp and set aside.
4. In the same skillet, add heavy cream and grated cheese. Stir until the sauce thickens.
5. Pour the cheese sauce over the shrimp before serving.

Nutritional Facts (Per Serving): Calories: 625 | Sugars: 2g | Fat: 45g | Carbs: 0g | Protein: 30g | Fiber: 0g | Sodium: 1000mg | Vitamin A: 200µg | Vitamin B1: 0.274mg | Vitamin B2: 0.274mg | Vitamin B3: 3.8mg NE | Vitamin B5: 1.24mg | Vitamin B6: 0.324mg | Vitamin B7: 7.3mg | Vitamin B9: 14µg | Vitamin B12: 2.6µg | Iron: 4.4mg | Zinc: 5mg

Roasted beef chunks and beef liver

Prep: 10 minutes | Cook: 25 minutes | Serves: 1

Ingredients:

- 4 oz beef chunks (120g)
- 4 oz beef liver (120g)
- 2 tbsp butter (30g)
- 1/4 cup beef gravy (60ml)
- Salt and pepper to taste

Instructions:

1. Preheat oven to 375°F (190°C).
2. Season beef chunks and liver with salt and pepper.
3. Heat butter in a skillet over medium-high heat. Sear beef chunks and liver until browned.
4. Transfer to a baking dish and roast in the oven for 15-20 minutes.
5. Serve with heated beef gravy.

Nutritional Information (Per Serving): Calories: 625 | Sugars: 0g | Fat: 43g | Carbs: 0g | Protein: 30g | Fiber: 0g | Sodium: 1000mg | Vitamin A: 220µg | Vitamin B1: 0.275mg | Vitamin B2: 0.275mg | Vitamin B3: 3.9mg NE | Vitamin B5: 1.25mg | Vitamin B6: 0.325mg | Vitamin B7: 7.4mg | Vitamin B9: 14µg | Vitamin B12: 2.7µg | Iron: 4.5mg | Zinc: 6mg

Pan-fried pork chunks with meat sauce and quail eggs

Prep: 10 minutes | Cook: 15 minutes | Serves: 1

Ingredients:

- 8 oz pork chunks (225g)
- 4 quail eggs (50g)
- 2 tbsp butter (30g)
- 1/4 cup meat sauce (60ml)
- Salt and pepper to taste

Instructions:

1. Heat butter in a skillet over medium heat.
2. Add pork chunks and cook until browned and cooked through, about 8-10 minutes.
3. In a separate skillet, fry quail eggs until whites are set, about 2-3 minutes.
4. Serve pork chunks topped with meat sauce and fried quail eggs.

Nutritional Facts (Per Serving): Calories: 625 | Sugars: 1g | Fat: 45g | Carbs: 0g | Protein: 29g | Fiber: 0g | Sodium: 1000mg | Vitamin A: 210µg | Vitamin B1: 0.275mg | Vitamin B2: 0.275mg | Vitamin B3: 3.7mg NE | Vitamin B5: 1.24mg | Vitamin B6: 0.324mg | Vitamin B7: 7.3mg | Vitamin B9: 13µg | Vitamin B12: 2.6µg | Iron: 4.4mg | Zinc: 5mg

Fish skillet with salmon and bacon

Prep: 10 minutes | Cook: 20 minutes | Serves: 1

Ingredients:

- 4 oz salmon fillet (120g)
- 4 slices bacon (120g)
- 2 tbsp butter (30g)
- 1/4 cup smoked bacon sauce (60ml)
- Salt and pepper to taste

Instructions:

1. Cook bacon in a skillet over medium heat until crispy. Remove and set aside.
2. In the same skillet, melt butter and add salmon fillet. Cook until opaque, about 4-5 minutes per side.
3. Pour smoked bacon sauce over the salmon and top with crispy bacon pieces.

Nutritional Facts (Per Serving): Calories: 625 | Sugars: 0g | Fat: 45g | Carbs: 0g | Protein: 30g | Fiber: 0g | Sodium: 1000mg | Vitamin A: 180µg | Vitamin B1: 0.273mg | Vitamin B2: 0.273mg | Vitamin B3: 3.5mg NE | Vitamin B5: 1.23mg | Vitamin B6: 0.323mg | Vitamin B7: 7.2mg | Vitamin B9: 13µg | Vitamin B12: 2.5µg | Iron: 4.3mg | Zinc: 4mg

CHAPTER 17: DINNER: Meaty dinners for every taste

Osso buco lamb shank

Prep: 15 minutes | Cook: 2 hours | Serves: 1

Ingredients:

- 1 lamb shank (14 oz / 400g)
- 3 tbsp bone marrow (45ml)
- Salt and pepper to taste

Instructions:

1. Season the lamb shank with salt and pepper.
2. Sear the lamb shank in a hot skillet until browned on all sides.
3. Add bone marrow and cover. Braise over low heat for 2 hours until tender.
4. Serve with the reduced braising liquid.

Nutritional Facts (Per Serving): Calories: 625 | Sugars: 0g | Fat: 45g | Carbs: 0g | Protein: 30g | Fiber: 0g | Sodium: 1000mg | Vitamin A: 200µg | Vitamin B1: 0.275mg | Vitamin B2: 0.275mg | Vitamin B3: 4mg NE | Vitamin B5: 1.25mg | Vitamin B6: 0.325mg | Vitamin B7: 7.5mg | Vitamin B9: 15µg | Vitamin B12: 2.7µg | Iron: 4.5mg | Zinc: 6mg

Herb-crusted rack of lamb

Prep: 10 minutes | Cook: 25 minutes | Serves: 1

Ingredients:

- 1 rack of lamb (12 oz / 340g)
- 2 tbsp pork fat (30g)
- Salt and pepper to taste

Instructions:

1. Preheat oven to 400°F (200°C).
2. Rub the lamb rack with pork fat and mixed herbs. Season with salt and pepper.
3. Bake in the oven for 20-25 minutes until crust is golden and meat is cooked to desired doneness.
4. Rest for 5 minutes before serving.

Nutritional Facts (Per Serving): Calories: 625 | Sugars: 0g | Fat: 45g | Carbs: 0g | Protein: 30g | Fiber: 0g | Sodium: 1000mg | Vitamin A: 225µg | Vitamin B1: 0.275mg | Vitamin B2: 0.275mg | Vitamin B3: 3.5mg NE | Vitamin B5: 1.23mg | Vitamin B6: 0.323mg | Vitamin B7: 7.2mg | Vitamin B9: 13µg | Vitamin B12: 2.5µg | Iron: 4.3mg | Zinc: 5mg

Chopped chicken cutlets

Prep: 10 minutes | Cook: 20 minutes | Serves: 1

Ingredients:

- 8 oz ground chicken (225g)
- 2 slices bacon (60g)
- 2 oz cheddar cheese, grated (60g)
- Salt and pepper to taste

Instructions:

1. Form ground chicken into patties.
2. Cook bacon in a skillet until crispy, remove and set aside.
3. In the same skillet, cook chicken patties until golden and cooked through, about 8-10 minutes per side.
4. Top with bacon and grated cheese, let the cheese melt before serving.

Nutritional Facts (Per Serving): Calories: 625 | Sugars: 0g | Fat: 45g | Carbs: 0g | Protein: 28g | Fiber: 0g | Sodium: 1000mg | Vitamin A: 180µg | Vitamin B1: 0.273mg | Vitamin B2: 0.273mg | Vitamin B3: 3.5mg NE | Vitamin B5: 1.23mg | Vitamin B6: 0.323mg | Vitamin B7: 7.2mg | Vitamin B9: 13µg | Vitamin B12: 2.5µg | Iron: 4.3mg | Zinc: 4mg

Beef chops with peppercorn sauce

Prep: 10 minutes | Cook: 15 minutes | Serves: 1

Ingredients:

- oz beef chops (225g)
- 1 tbsp black peppercorns, crushed (15g)
- 2 tbsp butter (30g)
- Salt to taste

Instructions:

1. Season beef chops with salt and crushed peppercorns.
2. Heat butter in a skillet over medium heat.
3. Cook beef chops until desired doneness, about 4-5 minutes per side.
4. Serve with melted butter and peppercorns from the skillet.

Nutritional Facts (Per Serving): Calories: 625 | Sugars: 0g | Fat: 45g | Carbs: 0g | Protein: 30g | Fiber: 0g | Sodium: 1000mg | Vitamin A: 200µg | Vitamin B1: 0.275mg | Vitamin B2: 0.275mg | Vitamin B3: 4mg NE | Vitamin B5: 1.25mg | Vitamin B6: 0.325mg | Vitamin B7: 7.5mg | Vitamin B9: 15µg | Vitamin B12: 2.7µg | Iron: 4.5mg | Zinc: 6mg

Beef ham in creamy glaze

Prep:15 minutes | Cook: 1 hour | Serves: 1

Ingredients:

- 10 oz beef ham (280g)
- 2 tbsp Hollandaise sauce (30ml)
- Salt and pepper to taste

Instructions:

1. Preheat oven to 375°F (190°C).
2. Season beef ham with salt and pepper.
3. Bake for 45 minutes until cooked through.
4. Brush with Hollandaise sauce and bake for an additional 15 minutes until glazed.
5. Serve hot.

Nutritional Facts (Per Serving): Calories: 625 | Sugars: 0g | Fat: 44g | Carbs: 0g | Protein: 29g | Fiber: 0g | Sodium: 1000mg | Vitamin A: 210µg | Vitamin B1: 0.274mg | Vitamin B2: 0.274mg | Vitamin B3: 3.6mg NE | Vitamin B5: 1.24mg | Vitamin B6: 0.324mg | Vitamin B7: 7.4mg | Vitamin B9: 14µg | Vitamin B12: 2.6µg | Iron: 4.4mg | Zinc: 5mg

Braised pork knuckle

Prep: 10 minutes | Cook: 2 hours | Serves: 1

Ingredients:

- 1 pork knuckle (14 oz / 400g)
- 2 slices bacon (60g)
- 2 tbsp butter (30g)
- Salt to taste

Instructions:

1. Season pork knuckle with salt.
2. Sear pork knuckle in a hot skillet until browned on all sides.
3. Add bacon and butter, cover, and braise over low heat for 2 hours until tender.
4. Serve with the reduced braising liquid.

Nutritional Facts (Per Serving): Calories: 625 | Sugars: 0g | Fat: 45g | Carbs: 0g | Protein: 30g | Fiber: 0g | Sodium: 1000mg | Vitamin A: 200µg | Vitamin B1: 0.275mg | Vitamin B2: 0.275mg | Vitamin B3: 4mg NE | Vitamin B5: 1.25mg | Vitamin B6: 0.325mg | Vitamin B7: 7.5mg | Vitamin B9: 15µg | Vitamin B12: 2.7µg | Iron: 4.5mg | Zinc: 6mg

Grilled beef tacos on egg pancakes

Prep: 15 minutes | Cook: 20 minutes | Serves: 1

Ingredients:

- 6 oz beef, grilled and sliced (170g)
- 2 large eggs (100g)
- 2 tbsp butter (30g)
- Salt and pepper to taste

Instructions:

1. Beat eggs and season with salt and pepper.
2. Cook eggs in butter to make thick pancakes.
3. Top egg pancakes with grilled beef slices.
4. Serve immediately.

Nutritional Facts (Per Serving): Calories: 625 | Sugars: 0g | Fat: 45g | Carbs: 0g | Protein: 28g | Fiber: 0g | Sodium: 1000mg | Vitamin A: 200µg | Vitamin B1: 0.273mg | Vitamin B2: 0.273mg | Vitamin B3: 3.5mg NE | Vitamin B5: 1.23mg | Vitamin B6: 0.323mg | Vitamin B7: 7.2mg | Vitamin B9: 13µg | Vitamin B12: 2.5µg | Iron: 4.3mg | Zinc: 4mg

Stuffed beef patties

Prep: 15 minutes | Cook: 25 minutes | Serves: 1

Ingredients:

- 8 oz ground beef (225g)
- 2 oz chicken liver or bacon, chopped (60g)
- 2 tbsp Peppercorn sauce (30ml)
- Salt and pepper to taste

Instructions:

1. Form ground beef into patties, stuffing each with chicken liver or bacon.
2. Cook patties in a skillet over medium heat until browned and cooked through, about 10-12 minutes per side.
3. Serve with Peppercorn sauce.

Nutritional Facts (Per Serving): Calories: 625 | Sugars: 0g | Fat: 44g | Carbs: 0g | Protein: 30g | Fiber: 0g | Sodium: 1000mg | Vitamin A: 220µg | Vitamin B1: 0.275mg | Vitamin B2: 0.275mg | Vitamin B3: 3.8mg NE | Vitamin B5: 1.25mg | Vitamin B6: 0.325mg | Vitamin B7: 7.5mg | Vitamin B9: 14µg | Vitamin B12: 2.7µg | Iron: 4.5mg | Zinc: 5mg

Wild salmon Wellington

Prep: 15 minutes | Cook: 25 minutes | Serves: 1

Ingredients:

- 1 salmon filet (7 oz / 200g)
- 2 oz pork fat (60g)
- 2 large eggs (100g)
- 2 oz cheddar cheese, grated (60g)
- Salt and pepper to taste

Instructions:

1. Preheat oven to 375°F (190°C).
2. Blend eggs, cheese and pork fat to form a creamy batter.
3. Wrap the salmon filet in the egg and pork fat batter.
4. Place on a baking sheet and bake for 25 minutes until golden brown.
5. Season with salt and pepper before serving.

Nutritional Facts (Per Serving): Calories: 625 | Sugars: 0g | Fat: 44g | Carbs: 0g | Protein: 30g | Fiber: 0g | Sodium: 1000mg | Vitamin A: 200µg | Vitamin B1: 0.275mg | Vitamin B2: 0.275mg | Vitamin B3: 3.5mg NE | Vitamin B5: 1.24mg | Vitamin B6: 0.325mg | Vitamin B7: 7.3mg | Vitamin B9: 14µg | Vitamin B12: 2.6µg | Iron: 4.4mg | Zinc: 5mg

Seared sea bass with butter and cheese sauce

Prep: 10 minutes | Cook: 15 minutes | Serves: 1

Ingredients:

- 1 sea bass filet (7 oz / 200g)
- 2 tbsp butter (30g)
- 2 oz grated cheese (60g)
- Salt to taste

Instructions:

1. Season the sea bass filet with salt.
2. Melt butter in a skillet over medium heat.
3. Sear the sea bass filet until golden brown, about 5-6 minutes per side.
4. Remove the filet and in the same pan, add grated cheese to the remaining butter. Stir until melted and smooth.
5. Serve the filet with the cheese sauce drizzled over.

Nutritional Facts (Per Serving): Calories: 625 | Sugars: 0g | Fat: 45g | Carbs: 0g | Protein: 29g | Fiber: 0g | Sodium: 1000mg | Vitamin A: 210µg | Vitamin B1: 0.274mg | Vitamin B2: 0.274mg | Vitamin B3: 3.8mg NE | Vitamin B5: 1.25mg | Vitamin B6: 0.324mg | Vitamin B7: 7.4mg | Vitamin B9: 13µg | Vitamin B12: 2.7µg | Iron: 4.5mg | Zinc: 6mg

Carp baked in sour cream

Prep: 10 minutes | Cook: 30 minutes | Serves: 1

Ingredients:

- 1 whole carp (14 oz / 400g)
- 4 oz sour cream (120g)
- Salt to taste

Instructions:

1. Preheat oven to 350°F (175°C).
2. Season the carp with salt and coat with sour cream.
3. Place the carp in a baking dish and bake for 30 minutes until cooked through.
4. Serve hot.

Nutritional Facts (Per Serving): Calories: 625 | Sugars: 1g | Fat: 43g | Carbs: 0g | Protein: 30g | Fiber: 0g | Sodium: 1000mg | Vitamin A: 225µg | Vitamin B1: 0.275mg | Vitamin B2: 0.275mg | Vitamin B3: 3.9mg NE | Vitamin B5: 1.23mg | Vitamin B6: 0.325mg | Vitamin B7: 7.5mg | Vitamin B9: 14µg | Vitamin B12: 2.5µg | Iron: 4.4mg | Zinc: 6mg

Canadian trout

Prep: 10 minutes | Cook: 20 minutes | Serves: 1

Ingredients:

- 1 whole trout (14 oz / 400g)
- 2 tbsp butter (30g)
- Salt and pepper to taste

Instructions:

1. Preheat oven to 375°F (190°C).
2. Season the trout with salt and pepper.
3. Place the trout on a baking sheet and dot with butter.
4. Bake for 20 minutes until the fish flakes easily with a fork.
5. Cut fish into nice slices and serve hot on a plate with hollandaise sauce and egg circles (optional).

Nutritional Facts (Per Serving): Calories: 625 | Sugars: 0g | Fat: 44g | Carbs: 0g | Protein: 30g | Fiber: 0g | Sodium: 1000mg | Vitamin A: 180µg | Vitamin B1: 0.273mg | Vitamin B2: 0.273mg | Vitamin B3: 3.7mg NE | Vitamin B5: 1.24mg | Vitamin B6: 0.323mg | Vitamin B7: 7.2mg | Vitamin B9: 13µg | Vitamin B12: 2.6µg | Iron: 4.3mg | Zinc: 4mg

CHAPTER 19 DINNER: Variety of steaks: from fish to game

Ribeye steak with cheese sauce

Prep: 10 minutes | Cook: 15 minutes | Serves: 1

Ingredients:

- 1 beef ribeye steak (8 oz / 225g)
- 1 pork ribeye steak (8 oz / 225g)
- 2 tbsp butter (30g)
- 1/4 cup cheese sauce (60ml)

Instructions:

1. Season the ribeye steaks .
2. Heat butter in a skillet over medium-high heat.
3. Sear the steaks in the skillet until golden brown, about 4-5 minutes per side.
4. Serve the steaks with cheese sauce or with cheese and shrimp (optional).

Nutritional Facts (Per Serving): Calories: 625 | Sugars: 1g | Fat: 45g | Carbs: 0g | Protein: 29g | Fiber: 0g | Sodium: 1000mg | Vitamin A: 200µg | Vitamin B1: 0.275mg | Vitamin B2: 0.275mg | Vitamin B3: 4mg NE | Vitamin B5: 1.25mg | Vitamin B6: 0.325mg | Vitamin B7: 7.5mg | Vitamin B9: 15µg | Vitamin B12: 2.7µg | Iron: 4.5mg | Zinc: 6mg

New York strip steak with shrimp butter

Prep: 10 minutes | Cook: 15 minutes | Serves: 1

Ingredients:

- 1 New York strip steak (10 oz / 280g)
- 2 tbsp shrimp butter (30g)

Instructions:

1. Heat a skillet over medium-high heat.
2. Sear the New York strip steak until desired doneness, about 4-5 minutes per side.
3. Top with shrimp butter and serve immediately.

Nutritional Facts (Per Serving): Calories: 625 | Sugars: 0g | Fat: 43g | Carbs: 0g | Protein: 30g | Fiber: 0g | Sodium: 1000mg | Vitamin A: 180µg | Vitamin B1: 0.273mg | Vitamin B2: 0.273mg | Vitamin B3: 3.5mg NE | Vitamin B5: 1.23mg | Vitamin B6: 0.323mg | Vitamin B7: 7.2mg | Vitamin B9: 13µg | Vitamin B12: 2.5µg | Iron: 4.3mg | Zinc: 4mg

Pork steak with mustard cream sauce

Prep: 10 minutes | Cook: 15 minutes | Serves: 1

Ingredients:

- 1 pork loin steak (8 oz / 225g)
- 1/4 cup heavy cream (60ml)
- 1 tbsp Dijon mustard (15g)

Instructions:

1. Grill the pork loin steak until cooked through, about 6-7 minutes per side.
2. In a small pan, combine heavy cream and Dijon mustard, heating until slightly thickened.
3. Serve the pork steak with mustard cream sauce.

Nutritional Facts (Per Serving): Calories: 625 | Sugars: 0g | Fat: 43g | Carbs: 0g | Protein: 30g | Fiber: 0g | Sodium: 1000mg | Vitamin A: 190µg | Vitamin B1: 0.274mg | Vitamin B2: 0.273mg | Vitamin B3: 3.6mg NE | Vitamin B5: 1.24mg | Vitamin B6: 0.324mg | Vitamin B7: 7.3mg | Vitamin B9: 14µg | Vitamin B12: 2.6µg | Iron: 4.4mg | Zinc: 4.5mg

Sirloin steak with pepper sauce

Prep: 10 minutes | Cook: 15 minutes | Serves: 1

Ingredients:

- 1 sirloin steak (8 oz / 225g)
- 1/4 cup Greek yogurt (60ml)
- 1 tbsp ground black pepper (15g)

Instructions:

1. Grill the sirloin steak until desired doneness, about 5-6 minutes per side.
2. In a bowl, mix Greek yogurt and ground black pepper.
3. Serve the steak with the pepper sauce.

Nutritional Facts (Per Serving): Calories: 625 | Sugars: 2g | Fat: 43g | Carbs: 0g | Protein: 30g | Fiber: 0g | Sodium: 1000mg | Vitamin A: 185µg | Vitamin B1: 0.274mg | Vitamin B2: 0.274mg | Vitamin B3: 3.6mg NE | Vitamin B5: 1.24mg | Vitamin B6: 0.324mg | Vitamin B7: 7.3mg | Vitamin B9: 14µg | Vitamin B12: 2.6µg | Iron: 4.4mg | Zinc: 4.5mg

Flat iron steak with meat sauce

Prep: 10 minutes | Cook: 20 minutes | Serves: 1

Ingredients:

- 1 flat iron steak (8 oz / 225g)
- 1/4 cup meat sauce (60ml)

Instructions:

1. Grill the flat iron steak until desired doneness, about 5-6 minutes per side.
2. Heat the meat sauce in a small pan.
3. Serve the steak with the meat sauce.

Nutritional Facts (Per Serving): Calories: 625 | Sugars: 0g | Fat: 43g | Carbs: 0g | Protein: 30g | Fiber: 0g | Sodium: 1000mg | Vitamin A: 180µg | Vitamin B1: 0.273mg | Vitamin B2: 0.273mg | Vitamin B3: 3.5mg NE | Vitamin B5: 1.23mg | Vitamin B6: 0.323mg | Vitamin B7: 7.2mg | Vitamin B9: 13µg | Vitamin B12: 2.5µg | Iron: 4.3mg | Zinc: 4mg

Tuna steak glazed with caviar sauce

Prep: 10 minutes | Cook: 10 minutes | Serves: 1

Ingredients:

- 1 tuna steak (6 oz / 170g)
- 2 tbsp caviar (30g)
- 1 tbsp butter (15g)

Instructions:

1. Grill the tuna steak until desired doneness, about 3-4 minutes per side.
2. Melt butter in a small pan and mix with caviar.
3. Glaze the tuna steak with the caviar sauce before serving.

Nutritional Facts (Per Serving): Calories: 625 | Sugars: 0g | Fat: 43g | Carbs: 0g | Protein: 30g | Fiber: 0g | Sodium: 1000mg | Vitamin A: 190µg | Vitamin B1: 0.274mg | Vitamin B2: 0.274mg | Vitamin B3: 3.6mg NE | Vitamin B5: 1.24mg | Vitamin B6: 0.324mg | Vitamin B7: 7.3mg | Vitamin B9: 14µg | Vitamin B12: 2.6µg | Iron: 4.4mg | Zinc: 4.5mg

Steak and kidney pie (Carnivore Diet Version)

Prep: 10 minutes | Cook: 2 hours | Serves: 1

Ingredients:

- 2.7 oz beef steak, cubed and lamb kidneys, chopped (75g each)
- 2 tsp beef tallow (10g)
- Salt and pepper to taste
- 1/4 cup beef broth (60ml)

Cheese and bacon crust
- 1 cup grated cheddar and mozzarella cheese (120g each)
- 4 slices cooked bacon, crumbled (60g)
- 1 large egg (50g)
- 2 tbsp cream cheese, softened (30g)
- Salt and pepper to taste

Instructions:

1. Preheat oven to 350°F (175°C).
2. Mix grated cheese, crumbled bacon, egg, and cream cheese in a bowl. Season with salt and pepper.
3. Spread the mixture into a greased pie dish, covering the bottom and sides. Reserve some for the top crust. Bake for 8-10 minutes until golden.
4. Slice beef and kidneys. Heat beef fat in a skillet and fry meat for 5-7 minutes. Add beef stock, salt, and pepper. Simmer for 10 minutes.
5. Transfer to the cheese crust, cover with reserved mixture, and bake for 1.5 hours.

Nutritional Facts (Per Serving): Calories: 625 | Sugars 0g | Fat: 43g | Carbs: 0g | Protein: 30g | Fiber: 0g | Sodium: 1000mg | Vitamin A: 180µg | Vitamin B1 0.274mg | Vitamin B2: 0.275mg | Vitamin B3: 3.6mg NE Vitamin B5: 1.24mg | Vitamin B6: 0.324mg | Vitamin B7 7.3mg | Vitamin B9: 14µg | Vitamin B12: 2.6µg | Iron 4.4mg | Zinc: 5mg

Turkey baked whole (Carnivore Diet Version)

Prep: 10 minutes | Cook: 3 hours | Serves: 1

Ingredients:

- 1 lb whole turkey (450g)
- 1 tbsp melted butter (15ml)
- Salt and pepper to taste

Instructions:

1. Preheat the oven to 325°F (165°C).
2. Brush the turkey with melted butter and season with salt and pepper. Place the turkey in a baking dish and cover loosely with foil.
3. Bake for 3 hours, basting occasionally, until internal temperature reaches 165°F (74°C). Let res for 20 minutes before carving.
4. Serve with your favorite sauces.

Nutritional Facts (Per Serving): Calories: 625 | Sugars 0g | Fat: 45g | Carbs: 0g | Protein: 29g | Fiber: 0g | Sodium: 1000mg | Vitamin A: 225µg | Vitamin B1

0.275mg | Vitamin B2: 0.275mg | Vitamin B3: 3.5mg NE | Vitamin B5: 1.25mg | Vitamin B6: 0.325mg | Vitamin B7: 7.5mg | Vitamin B9: 15µg | Vitamin B12: 2.7µg | Iron: 4.5mg | Zinc: 6mg

Baked beef with rosemary oil (Carnivore Diet Version)

Prep: 10 minutes | Cook: 1.5 hours | Serves: 1

Ingredients:

- 7 oz beef roast (200g)
- 1 tbsp butter (15g)
- Salt and pepper to taste

Instructions:

1. Preheat oven to 350°F (175°C).
2. Rub the beef with butter and season with salt and pepper.
3. Place in a small roasting pan and roast for 1.5 hours, or until desired doneness.
4. Let rest for 15 minutes before slicing.

Nutritional Facts (Per Serving): Calories: 625 | Sugars: 0g | Fat: 44g | Carbs: 0g | Protein: 30g | Fiber: 0g | Sodium: 1000mg | Vitamin A: 200µg | Vitamin B1: 0.274mg | Vitamin B2: 0.273mg | Vitamin B3: 3.7mg NE | Vitamin B5: 1.23mg | Vitamin B6: 0.324mg | Vitamin B7: 7.2mg | Vitamin B9: 13µg | Vitamin B12: 2.5µg | Iron: 4.3mg | Zinc: 5mg

Butter braised grouse, capon, or teal duck (Carnivore Diet Version)

Prep: 15 minutes | Cook: 1 hours | Serves: 1

Ingredients:

- 1 grouse, capon, or teal duck (1 lb / 450g)
- 2 tbsp butter (30g)
- Salt and pepper to taste

Instructions:

1. Preheat oven to 375°F (190°C).
2. Melt butter in a skillet over medium heat.
3. Sear bird until browned, about 5 minutes per side.
4. Transfer to a small baking dish, pour melted butter over, and season with salt and pepper.
5. Bake for 45 minutes to 1 hour until cooked through.

Nutritional Facts (Per Serving): Calories: 625 | Sugars: 0g | Fat: 43g | Carbs: 0g | Protein: 30g | Fiber: 0g | Sodium: 1000mg | Vitamin A: 200µg | Vitamin B1: 0.275mg | Vitamin B2: 0.275mg | Vitamin B3: 3.5mg NE | Vitamin B5: 1.25mg | Vitamin B6: 0.325mg | Vitamin B7: 7.5mg | Vitamin B9: 15µg | Vitamin B12: 2.7µg | Iron: 4.5mg | Zinc: 6mg

BBQ Pork ribs (Carnivore Diet Version)

Prep: 15 minutes | Cook: 2 hours | Serves: 1

Ingredients:

- 8 oz pork ribs (225g)
- 2 tbsp BBQ sauce (30ml, low carb sweetener)
- Salt and pepper to taste

Instructions:

1. Preheat oven to 300°F (150°C).
2. Season ribs with salt and pepper.
3. Wrap ribs in foil and bake for 2 hours until tender.
4. Brush with BBQ sauce and grill for 5-10 minutes until caramelized.

Nutritional Facts (Per Serving): Calories: 625 | Sugars: 2g | Fat: 44g | Carbs: 0g | Protein: 29g | Fiber: 0g | Sodium: 1000mg | Vitamin A: 180µg | Vitamin B1: 0.275mg | Vitamin B2: 0.273mg | Vitamin B3: 3.6mg NE | Vitamin B5: 1.23mg | Vitamin B6: 0.325mg | Vitamin B7: 7.3mg | Vitamin B9: 13µg | Vitamin B12: 2.6µg | Iron: 4.4mg | Zinc: 5mg

Carnivore-friendly beef Wellington (Carnivore Diet Version)

Prep: 30 minutes | Cook: 1 hours | Serves: 1

Ingredients:

- 1 cup grated cheddar, mozzarella cheese (120g each)
- 1 cup chicken pate (120g)
- 4 slices cooked bacon, crumbled (60g)
- 1 large egg (50g)
- 2 tbsp cream cheese, softened (30g)
- Salt and pepper to taste

Instructions:

1. Preheat oven to 400°F (200°C).
2. Sear beef tenderloin in butter until browned, about 5 minutes.
3. Spread chicken liver pate over beef.
4. Wrap beef in prosciutto and a layer of grated cheese; place in a small baking dish.
5. Bake for 25-30 minutes until internal temperature reaches 125°F (52°C) for medium-rare.
6. Let rest for 10 minutes before slicing.

Nutritional Facts (Per Serving): Calories: 625 | Sugars: 0g | Fat: 43g | Carbs: 0g | Protein: 30g | Fiber: 0g | Sodium: 1000mg | Vitamin A: 225µg | Vitamin B1: 0.273mg | Vitamin B2: 0.275mg | Vitamin B3: 3.5mg NE | Vitamin B5: 1.25mg | Vitamin B6: 0.325mg | Vitamin B7: 7.5mg | Vitamin B9: 15µg | Vitamin B12: 2.7µg | Iron: 4.5mg | Zinc: 6mg

Streamlined Shopping and Meal Planning: Tailored Tools for Your Carnivore Journey

To enhance your experience with the Carnivore Diet, we've developed a comprehensive 30-day grocery shopping guide specifically aligned with our cookbook. This guide is designed to make meal preparation effortless by focusing on high-quality animal products and reducing reliance on processed foods. Pay close attention to hidden carbohydrates and sugars, particularly in processed meats or any additives. Modify quantities based on your personal dietary needs, all while maintaining the Carnivore Diet's emphasis on meat-based, high-protein, and high-fat nutrients. Begin your journey towards simple, satisfying, and health-boosting eating with confidence!

Grocery Shopping List for 7-Day Meal Plan

Meat and Poultry
Bacon: 2 lbs (900g)
Eggs: 4 dozen (approx. 48 eggs)
Ribeye Steaks: 4 large steaks (approx. 2 lbs or 900g each)
Ground Beef: 2 lbs (900g) for Beef Tartare and Beef Muffins
Lamb Shanks: 2-4 shanks for Osso Buco
Pork Zrazy: 1.5 lbs (680g) ground pork
Pork Chops: 2 lbs (900g)
Chicken Thighs: 2 lbs (900g)
Beef Liver: 1 lb (450g) for Creamy Chicken Liver Soup
Beef Cutlets: 2 lbs (900g)
Pork Ribs: 2 lbs (900g) for BBQ Pork Ribs
Quail Eggs: 1 dozen (for Quail Eggs in Butter)
Ham: 0.5 lb (225g) for Cheese Balls with Slices of Boiled Ham
Lamb Rack: 1 rack for Herb-Crusted Rack of Lamb
Pork and Lamb Kebab: 1 lb (450g) each of pork and lamb
Fish and Seafood
Haddock Fillets: 1 lb (450g)

for Haddock and Egg Fritters
Sea Bass Fillets: 1 lb (450g) for Seared Sea Bass
Salmon or Tuna Steaks: 1 lb (450g) for Tuna Steak Glazed with Caviar Sauce
Seafood Mix (shrimp, scallops, etc.): 2 lbs (900g) for Seafood Chowder
Dairy
Cheese:
Cheddar: 1 lb (450g)
Parmesan: 0.5 lb (225g)
Cream Cheese: 0.5 lb (225g)
Feta Cheese: 0.5 lb (225g)
Butter: 2 lbs (900g)
Heavy Cream: 2 pints (1 liter)
Cottage Cheese: 1 lb (450g)
Pantry Staples
Beef Broth: 4 cups (1 liter) for soups and sauces
Olive Oil: 1 bottle (500ml)
Red Wine Vinegar: 1 bottle (250ml) for sauces and dressings
Garlic: 2 heads
Onions: 4 large
Herbs and Spices:
Black Pepper
Salt (Sea Salt or Kosher Salt)
Paprika
Thyme
Rosemary
Bay Leaves
Peppercorns
Caviar (for Tuna Steak glaze)

Miscellaneous
Caviar: Small jar for Tuna Steak Glaze
Wood Chips: For BBQ Pork Ribs (if grilling)

Grocery Shopping List for 8-14 Day Meal Plan

Meat and Poultry
Beef:
Ground Beef: 2 lbs (900g) for Meatloaf with Cheese Sauce
Baked Beef: 2 lbs (900g) for Baked Beef in Yogurt
Roast Beef: 2 lbs (900g) for Classic Roast Beef
Beef Medallions: 2 lbs (900g) for Pepper-Crusted Beef Medallions
Beef Bones: 2 lbs (900g) for Beef Bone Broth
Pork:
Pork Belly: 1 lb (450g) for Pork Belly Breakfast
Pork Roll: 2 lbs (900g) for Pork Roll with Chicken and Cheese
Pork Stew: 2 lbs (900g) for Pork Stew
Pork Sausage: 1 lb (450g) for Egg and Cheese Tacos
Chicken:
Chicken Fillet: 2 lbs (900g) for

Chicken Fillet and Feta Cheese Omelet and Chicken Fricassee
Chicken Thighs: 2 lbs (900g) for Chopped Chicken Cutlets
Ground Chicken: 1 lb (450g) for Meatloaf
Lamb:
Rack of Lamb: 1 rack for Herb-Crusted Rack of Lamb
Eggs: 4 dozen (approx. 48 eggs) for various breakfasts and dishes
Grouse or Game Bird: 1 whole for Butter-Braised Grouse
Fish and Seafood
Salmon Fillets: 2 lbs (900g) for Wild Salmon Wellington and Salmon Tartare
White Fish (e.g., Haddock or Cod): 1 lb (450g) for Fish Fingers in Egg Batter and Fish Stew
Sea Bass Fillets: 1 lb (450g) for Seared Sea Bass
Caviar: Small jar for Seared Sea Bass with Butter and Cheese Sauce
Dairy
Butter: 2 lbs (900g)
Cheddar Cheese: 1 lb (450g) for various dishes
Feta Cheese: 0.5 lb (225g) for Chicken Fillet and Feta Cheese Omelet
Cream Cheese: 0.5 lb (225g)
Mascarpone Cheese: 0.5 lb (225g)
Cottage Cheese: 1 lb (450g)
Yogurt (Full-fat, unsweetened): 2 cups (500ml) for Baked Beef in Yogurt
Pantry Staples
Olive Oil: 1 bottle (500ml)
Red Wine Vinegar: 1 bottle (250ml)
Garlic: 2 heads
Onions: 4 large
Herbs and Spices:
Black Pepper
Salt (Sea Salt or Kosher Salt)
Paprika
Thyme
Rosemary
Bay Leaves

Peppercorns
Miscellaneous
Coconut Oil: 1 jar (for cooking if needed)
Cooking Spray: Optional, for easier cooking and cleanup
Fresh Herbs: Optional, for garnish and additional flavor in various dishes

Grocery Shopping List for 15-21 Day Meal Plan

Meat and Poultry
Chicken:
Chicken Fillet: 2 lbs (900g) for Chicken Fillet with Raw Smoked Sausage and Fried Egg-Breaded Chicken Fillet
Chicken Thighs: 2 lbs (900g) for Chicken Thighs with Creamy Sauce
Chicken Breast: 1 lb (450g) for Chicken Bone Broth
Raw Smoked Sausage: 1 lb (450g) for Chicken Fillet with Raw Smoked Sausage
Ground Chicken: 1 lb (450g) for Chicken Pudding
Bacon: 2 lbs (900g) for Bacon-Wrapped Shrimp Skewers and Bacon Egg Muffins
Beef:
Ribeye Steak: 2 lbs (900g) for Ribeye Steak with Cheese Sauce
Ground Beef: 1 lb (450g) for Grilled Beef Tacos
Beef Tongue: 2 lbs (900g) for Braised Beef Tongue
Beef Bones: 2 lbs (900g) for Cream Soup of Beef and Cheese and Chicken Bone Broth
Beef Strips or Steaks: 2 lbs (900g) for Cheese and Egg Burrito with Steak and Bacon
Ribeye Steak: 2 lbs (900g) for Ribeye Steak with

Cheese Sauce
Beef for Soufflé: 1 lb (450g) for Meat Soufflé
Pork:
Pork Chops: 2 lbs (900g) for Cream Pork Chops
Pork Lard: 1 lb (450g) for Pork Lard Chimichurri
Pork Steaks: 2 lbs (900g) for Pork Steak with Mustard Cream Sauce
Ground Pork: 1 lb (450g) for Stuffed Turkey Patties
Bacon: 1 lb (450g) for Bacon-Wrapped Shrimp Skewers
Pork Ham: 1 lb (450g) for Cheese Balls with Slices of Boiled Ham
Turkey:
Turkey Breast: 1 lb (450g) for Stuffed Turkey Patties
Turkey Slices: 1 lb (450g) for Turkey Tubes with Bacon
Lamb:
Lamb for Ragu: 2 lbs (900g) for Lamb Ragu Italian-Style
Shrimp: 1 lb (450g) for Bacon-Wrapped Shrimp Skewers
Tuna: 1 lb (450g) for Tuna Steak Glazed with Caviar Sauce
Fish and Seafood
Salmon Fillets: 1 lb (450g) for Baked Salmon with Herb Crust
Sea Bass Fillets: 1 lb (450g) for Seared Sea Bass
Shrimp: 1 lb (450g) for Bacon-Wrapped Shrimp Skewers
Caviar: Small jar for Tuna Steak Glazed with Caviar Sauce
Dairy
Butter: 2 lbs (900g)
Cheddar Cheese: 1 lb (450g)
Cream Cheese: 0.5 lb (225g)
Feta Cheese: 0.5 lb (225g) for Chicken Fillet and Feta Cheese Omelet
Cottage Cheese: 1 lb (450g) for Cottage Cheese Casserole with Cream

Mascarpone Cheese: 0.5 lb (225g) for various dishes
Eggs: 4 dozen (approx. 48 eggs) for various breakfasts and dishes
Heavy Cream: 1 pint (500ml) for various dishes
Pantry Staples
Olive Oil: 1 bottle (500ml)
Red Wine Vinegar: 1 bottle (250ml)
Garlic: 2 heads
Onions: 4 large
Herbs and Spices:
Black Pepper
Salt (Sea Salt or Kosher Salt)
Paprika
Thyme
Rosemary
Bay Leaves
Peppercorns
Miscellaneous
Coconut Oil: 1 jar (for cooking if needed)
Cooking Spray: Optional, for easier cooking and cleanup
Fresh Herbs: Optional, for garnish and additional flavor in various dishes

Grocery Shopping List for 22-28 Day Meal Plan

Meat and Poultry
Beef:
Ground Beef: 1 lb (450g) for Beef Forshmak
Beef Cutlets: 2 lbs (900g) for Baked Beef in Yogurt
Ribeye Steaks: 2 lbs (900g) for Ribeye Steak with Cheese Sauce
Beef Tongue: 2 lbs (900g) for Braised Beef Tongue
Beef for Stuffed Pork Zrazy: 1 lb (450g)
Roast Beef: 2 lbs (900g) for Baked Beef with Rosemary Oil
Pork:

Pork Zrazy: 1 lb (450g)
Pork Knuckle: 2 lbs (900g) for Braised Pork Knuckle
Pork Roll: 1 lb (450g) for Pork Roll with Chicken and Cheese
Pork Belly: 1 lb (450g) for Deep-Fried Pork
Pork Ribs: 2 lbs (900g) for BBQ Pork Ribs
Pork for Cheese Balls: 1 lb (450g) for Cheese Balls with Slices of Boiled Ham
Chicken:
Chicken Thighs: 1 lb (450g) for Crispy Chicken Tabaka
Chicken Fillet: 2 lbs (900g) for Chicken Fricassee and Chicken Bone Broth with Egg and Chicken Breast
Chicken Breast: 1 lb (450g) for various dishes
Raw Chicken for Pork Roll: 1 lb (450g)
Turkey:
Turkey Breast: 1 lb (450g) for Turkey and Cheddar Casserole
Fish and Seafood:
Sea Bass Fillets: 1 lb (450g) for Seared Sea Bass with Butter and Cheese Sauce
Wild Salmon: 1 lb (450g) for Wild Salmon Wellington and Quail Eggs with Carpaccio from Smoked Wild Salmon
Tuna Steaks: 1 lb (450g) for Tuna Steak Glazed with Caviar Sauce
Shrimp: 1 lb (450g) for Bacon-Wrapped Shrimp Skewers
Haddock or White Fish Fillets: 1 lb (450g) for Fish Fingers in Egg Batter
Quail Eggs: 2 dozen (approx. 24 eggs) for Quail Eggs with Carpaccio
Dairy and Cheese
Cheese:
Cheddar Cheese: 1 lb (450g) for Turkey and Cheddar Casserole
Cream Cheese: 0.5 lb (225g)

for various dishes
Feta Cheese: 0.5 lb (225g) for different casseroles
Butter: 2 lbs (900g) for various recipes
Cottage Cheese: 1 lb (450g) for various dishes
Mascarpone Cheese: 0.5 lb (225g) for various dishes
Eggs: 5 dozen (approx. 60 eggs) for breakfasts, snacks, and sauces
Heavy Cream: 1 pint (500ml) for sauces and casseroles
Ricotta Cheese: 0.5 lb (225g) for Turkey and Cheddar Casserole
Pantry Staples
Olive Oil: 1 bottle (500ml) for cooking and sauces
Red Wine Vinegar: 1 bottle (250ml) for Hollandaise Sauce and marinades
Garlic: 2 heads for flavoring various dishes
Onions: 4 large for soups and stews
Herbs and Spices:
Black Pepper
Salt (Sea Salt or Kosher Salt)
Paprika
Rosemary (fresh or dried)
Thyme (fresh or dried)
Bay Leaves
Peppercorns
Smoked Paprika for various recipes
Miscellaneous
Coconut Oil: 1 jar (for frying and additional cooking if needed)
Cooking Spray: Optional, for easier cooking and cleanup
Caviar: Small jar for Tuna Steak Glazed with Caviar Sauce
Fresh Herbs: Optional, for garnish and additional flavor in various dishes

Made in the USA
Monee, IL
09 December 2024

72550003R00046